Swim Like a Fish

An easy guide
to developing self-leadership

Florence Dambricourt

First published June 2019

Copyright © 2019 Florence Dambricourt

ISBN-13: 978-2-9701330-0-1

Typeset in Times New Roman (font size 11)

Cover by Aimee Coveney (www.authordesignstudio.com)
Editing by Sian Phillips (www.sianphillips.com)

For cool packages on developing self-leadership, take a swim at
https://afishonahill.com/ or **https://talking4good.com/**

Here you are, a fish among many fishes,
living in an aquarium; a very simple one.
Four walls, water, more or less clear.

Still an aquarium. A set of walls linked to
your education, your place of birth, your social upbringing,
your emotions, your experiences, your dreams,
your decisions, and your actions.

What if you could widen that aquarium?
What if every single day you could push the walls further?
What if one day the aquarium was the sea; the ocean?

Welcome to Swim Like a Fish!
An easy guide to developing self-leadership.
Widen the aquarium, crack the walls
and explore the oceans.

FOREWORD

Gosh, it's been some eleven years since Florence and I first met at a mediators' conference. In Dublin as I recall. What struck me almost immediately was her open and curious mindset, her genuine interest in people, their behaviour and language and her desire to make a positive contribution to an individual's journey to his or her full potential.

As a result of that meeting and our shared values and beliefs, we co-authored a book together – *Building Bridges, Embracing NLP for Better Mediation,* and went on to co-deliver a communication workshop at a European Mediation and Coaching Conference in Edinburgh.

Through her subsequent work and research, Florence has discovered how self-talk, limiting self-beliefs and emotional choice completely affect our behaviour and hence our outcomes.

From my own work and practice as an international coach, writer and trainer I am convinced we are all going through a period of unprecedented change in the world and we cannot lead ourselves or others by reflecting on past experiences alone.

In this sense, self-leadership means being autonomous—not a slave to your past but able to reflect on your own biography with a degree of attachment. As an individual, the behaviour that got you to where you are today will not take you into the emerging future, and the person you are today is not the person you will be in that future. As the old is dying, so the new is waiting to be born. That change requires us to connect to our own emerging self because the issues on the outside are a mirror of the issues on the inside.

The keys to the future, then, lie within us.

Yet it is not enough to lead or manage in the context of symptoms and structures alone. We need to start at a deeper personal level to change our existing thoughts and to connect with our deeper sources of creativity and imagination. We need to come from a different internal source.

In this book Florence has seamlessly woven her academic research, esoteric thinking, and proven practice, into an invitational journey to discover your own higher future-self—the person you were meant to be—and hence, live the life you were meant to live.

Her starting position presupposes we are all leaders and that you are already the person you want to be. Now you just have to meet that person. Self-leadership, then, requires an ability to reflect on our own strengths and weaknesses, and to act in a way consistent with our own sense of who we are.

I like her paradox that we are all the same, and that is what allows us to be unique and special.

One of the gifts in this book is that Florence does not just tell us *what* to do, but creates the mindset, conditions and activities for each of us to walk our own journey of self-discovery—the *how* to do it. Her seven myths challenge us to recognise and question our previous thoughts and habits. Her link to cybernetics and system thinking leads us to reconnect with both the parts and whole of who we are now, by inviting us to sense and see authentic selves.

This book is essentially a quest in which you are the hero. You can decide to go in whichever direction you think is appropriate for you. You can dive into dark, forbidding places, stay in the comfort of what is familiar, stride confidently or tread hesitantly. All of it is invitational. Go at your own pace in your own direction. All you have to do now is accept her invitation to enter the oceans, for in these oceans is the treasure you seek.

Trevor Horne

devoncoach@live.com
www.devoncoach.com

As the Buddha said, 'I have shown you the path. It is up to you to travel the path'

– Matthieu Ricard [extract from Destructive Emotions (*A Scientific Dialogue with the Dalai Lama*, narrated by Daniel Goleman)]

Table of Contents

INTRODUCTION

How would you like to feel at peace; calm and serene on a daily basis? How would you enjoy knowing that whatever comes your way, you will handle it fine? Even better, what if you knew you could turn anything around, changing any event into an opportunity? How would it feel swimming through life, either surfing the waves or lost at the bottom, knowing you always have resources to keep your chosen direction, your head above water, and the waves to push you forward?

Welcome to the world of possibilities offered by self-leadership.

Self-leadership is having a developed sense of who we are, what we can do, and where we are going; coupled with the ability to influence our communication, emotions and behaviours on the way there.[1]

When we think about what we can do, we can go straight to setting ourselves goals and objectives; or we can take a more easy-going approach, looking only for directions, and then setting ourselves a horizon and an intention instead. We will explore each of these different aspects in due time, and we will see that we can easily interweave them depending on what we can do and where we are going to.

But, first a bit more on the journey you are about to embark on. It's not just *any* kind of journey; it's a spiralling one. Every day, you will discover or re-discover some crucial knowledge. You will then strengthen associated skills and begin to build step-by-step true competency in self-leadership.

Yes, it means daily practice. And yes, it means making the time to do something every day.

Let's say you have just learned to swim. You kind of understand the breast-stroke but you're still quite clumsy, and gliding on the water is a weird concept. Would you then immediately decide to cross the Atlantic as a solo swimmer?

Hmm ... Of course not! We do have some common sense and we know we would need a lot of training first. With this easy guide to developing self-leadership you are going to train your **brain muscles** and, like any muscles, they are going to need energy (food), exercise, rest and repetition through daily practice.

In fact, you are even going to modify the structure of your brain, but let's leave that piece of information for later in the journey.

There is another great advantage of daily practice. It helps when building up habits. And using self-leadership is a must-have habit nowadays. By reading this book, you are going to develop specific skills reaching competency levels in self-leadership, and together we are going to turn these skills into habits.

A few pages into the book, once your foundations have been established with our first three chapters, you will begin to notice an incredible change. Your mind will spontaneously tune in to pause and apply self-leadership skills naturally. As you reach self-leadership level two you will notice an even greater change; a feeling of peace as you strengthen your competency.

Ready to embark on this spiralling journey through oceans?

Ready to swim like a fish?

Organised into eleven chapters, this book takes you through eleven stages of growth in your personal leadership skills. Each chapter is split into seven swims, and each swim finishes with a practice exercise. To ensure the building up of the habits we are looking for, I suggest a swim a day.

When you feel you have established a strong foundation, you may swim faster. When you feel a skill is lacking strength, simply go back a few swims, re-establish the foundation, and practice, practice, practice. When reaching the end of each chapter, you will find extra exercises – *Some extra swimming for the highly motivated* – and a space to step back and collect your thoughts throughout your evolution.

The chosen learning approach is inductive; from specifics to general. Each swim focuses on specific elements or skills, which may have been either underused or used with a different focus. Each skill has several layers and we are going to build onto each layer. This is the spiralling effect.

You may decide to try exploring several chapters at once. If this is the right speed for you, go for it! Just make sure you ask yourself regularly: "Am I getting the best out of each of the swims?"

Trust your answers and adapt the speed in which you go through this easy guide. Remember you are changing your brain here. An extra five minutes on an exercise can save you five hours or even five months in becoming strong when applying either a new skill or an old one in a new way.

A short and important note: this book is neither a doctor nor a shrink, or even an artificial intelligence version of them. Exercises include body movements, possible stretches, mind exercises such as self-reflection, and brainstorming or thinking outside the box.

Do only what is comfortable for you. If necessary, check with your physician about any exercises – either physical or mental – that you are unsure about. Your physician will be able to advise if parallel support can add to your evolution. With this book you are going to coach yourself. Similar to any coaching program, it is important that you acknowledge that every action taken or decided upon when reading this book is your own choice and responsibility.

Developing self-leadership is a whole body and mind practice as well as a fascinating journey through vast oceans. Ready to let the fish in you swim?

1, Seven Useful Observations

I believe that you can always learn from observation.

– Tamara Tunie

Fish to fish

Before we get started you need one more thing. You need to decide where to record your thoughts and notes from the exercises. Ideally you'll want a notebook. It can be a good old-fashioned notebook with actual pages – then you need a pen as well. Or it can be a digital notebook – with a stylus. But it has to be a place dedicated to your decision to develop your competency in self-leadership.

You have it now?

It's handy and you can easily write on it?

Excellent!

How would you describe your chosen notebook? What would you observe about it?

Observations are extremely interesting.

An observation is, after all, factual information visible in plain sight. But here we are, going round and round in circles in our aquariums; where we think, we believe, we assume, we conclude, we forget, we run. And often, we are so busy doing all that, we stop seeing what is just there in front of us: the facts, the irrefutable observations.

What if we had an off-switch in our aquarium?

And we do – it's there in the corner. Push it now, slowing the water down … slower and slower. It feels like the slow motion replay you see on TV sports footage showing who has really touched the edge of the pool first. And you see once more, every single one of your moves; everything, from attitudes to perspectives and what makes up the world around you.

Swim 1: Observation, a forgotten skill

It's going so slowly. For the first time, you can truly observe every single thing around you. A tree visible through the window. A traffic light turning to green. Rain drops on the window. A smaller street than you remember to the right of the building opposite. Your colleague wearing a blue jumper. You notice sounds as well. The chatter of people passing by. A car breaking down. Maybe you're in your office. Maybe in your living room, sitting in your most comfortable chair. Wherever you are, while you're reading these lines, stop and break your usual pattern. Pause, raise your eyes, and look around for three things you have not noticed yet.

Yes, three things. Go on then.

To do so you had to look around. Then you had to ask yourself if you had already observed each item you saw. And next, you had to agree with yourself whether each specific observation could be added to the list. You may even have surprised yourself by noticing something unexpected. More importantly, you practiced the skill of observation; and it probably felt quite easy to do.

You may have observed mainly with your eyes; or you could have explored with your ears, your skin, and your nose as well. There are many ways to observe; each one engaging our brain differently and each one providing factual information. Observation is about gathering factual information. And it's a fundamental skill of self-leadership. One could even argue observation is one of the pillars of self-leadership.

Tip and Practice, Swim 1

The Tip! You already have the skill of observation. In fact, you already have the abilities and skills of self-leadership. You may have just forgotten to use them recently or even forgotten how to use them altogether.

The Practice! On a daily basis, take a moment to focus on using one specific sense. For instance, choose to close your eyes and then focus on hearing every sound around you. Or put earplugs in and then look at everything around. Or, closing your eyes again, assess what is around you using sensations on your skin. Each day, choose a different sense to observe with. Note which sense feels easier or more spontaneous.

Swim 2: Autonomy, another forgotten skill

The off-switch is still engaged. In your aquarium life is going like a slow-motion movie. And you're fine with it. After all, you pushed the off-switch. You were given an option: you took it. You applied autonomy.

Autonomy is a beautiful word; like a gift full of promises and ready to be unwrapped. Behind the word autonomy we find the ability of a person to make his or her own decisions. And to make your own decision is an act of self-leadership.

Do we spontaneously know about autonomy? Is it something we learn?

Am I already using the skill of autonomy?

Here we are, about to be born. Mum and Dad are enjoying their movie night, ready to snooze on the sofa. But then, stubborn as hell, we kick everything into action, without anyone telling us to do so. Furthermore, once born, we go on again, crying as loudly and as early as possible. And this is only the beginning. In the following weeks, even when our parents are exhausted, begging us to stop, we go on, raising our little voices, again and again. Has anyone asked us to do that? No. Then we start folding our hands into tiny fists, developing finger muscles, spontaneously closing, opening our fingers up, experimenting. Has anyone asked us to do that? No. One day, we choose to grab that table pulling ourselves up, using these ab muscles we have been building up when crawling on the floor. Has anyone asked us to do that? No. In fact, from the moment we are born we were developing our autonomy – I can walk – I can eat on my own – I can dress. And all these small actions leading to autonomy are acts of self-leadership.

Tip and Practice, Swim 2

The Tip! We are all born self-leaders with an innate[2] ability to develop autonomy. But, as we explore the world, we may have simply applied autonomy to the wrong actions; building an aquarium rather than swimming freely in open water.

The Practice! On a daily basis, note how often you perform actions over which you have full autonomy, e.g. choosing your clothes, drinking a glass of water, eating an apple … And yes, you are going to find many.

Swim 3: You know you're the boss

Let's pause for a moment. Keep reading these lines and, as you do so, roll your shoulders up and down a few times. Maybe sit a bit deeper in your chair or sofa. And get everything organised so you feel safe enough to close your eyes.

Nearly there? As you finish reading this paragraph, and in your own time, close your eyes for 5-10 seconds. You can count if that helps. Do it now as you finish reading this sentence.

How was it?

Did you close your eyes? Or did someone come and pull your eyelids closed for you?

Did you leave them open and keep on reading this swim?

Can we agree that an action has happened – and you made the decision to take that action? The text suggested something and you decided to follow the suggestion. Or maybe you didn't. In this specific case you were your own boss.

At times, we may have the impression that we don't choose our own actions and, yes at times, choices are imposed on us. Still we remain the boss of our reactions to whatever comes our way. It is challenging to be the boss. It can be scary, tiring, stressful, rich in emotions, full of excitement, a gift, a chore, an opportunity, extremely rewarding, and much more. It also gets easier the more we do it. It is essentially another layer to autonomy.

Tip and Practice, Swim 3

The Tip! You are always the boss of you.

The Practice! Following from our practice Swim 2, still on a daily basis, keep track of the actions where you feel you are the boss. These are actions you have decided to do by yourself. You are going to find many. And you are going to find many similar to what you saw with practice Swim 2. If you feel unsure whether you're the boss in some actions you've undertaken, list them with a question mark in brackets. We will come back to them later.

Swim 4: We have a body

In order to practice self-leadership, we do need a *self* to lead. It would help, right?

I don't know about you, but I have no idea what my *self* really is. That situation has a clear advantage. As long as I do not know what my *self* is, it can be anything, and the possibilities remain limitless. I often know what my *self* is not – for instance it is not a tree or a car. I usually know what my *self* is doing – for instance typing on a laptop keyboard. And I know my *self* has a body.

You have one as well; a body.

You may not see it yet as the perfect body for you, still it's a body. And it is likely to be made up of oxygen, hydrogen, nitrogen, calcium, phosphorous, some potassium, sulphur, sodium, chlorine and magnesium. It probably contains a brain, a heart, a set of guts, etc. As we speak, it generates electricity; several types of waves – acoustic – electromagnetics – thermic. And it has a mind of its own. As you read this page, your body is minding its own business, breathing in, breathing out, keeping warm, etc. Your body is actually good at self-leadership on its own. More than that, your body can influence how you apply self-leadership with your head. In time, one of our challenges is going to get both body and mind acting with the same intention in their self-leadership.

What is this body first of all? A sign we are here? A proof we exist? Something we can touch or grab? It is our physical presence, like an anchor, and we want to make this anchor very strong.

Tip and Practice, Swim 4

The Tip! Your body is like an anchor in today's world. A very important anchor which we want robust and strong.

The Practice! How is your body at the moment? Can you feel tension or relaxation in your muscles? Can you close your hands and then release them? Can you now feel your back against the chair? What about your feet? What happens when you press your feet on the floor? Note how focusing on your body and its interaction with your surroundings makes your physical presence stronger. You're therefore anchoring your body.

Swim 5: We can breathe as well

Okay. Our body is our physical presence, and through this physical presence it gives us a lot of information about us being here, in this room, at this specific time, reading these lines.

Let's make this body talk louder. Fold your hands together for a moment and feel your knuckles against each other. Now put your hands on your thighs and focus on feeling the heat building up under your hands. Put one hand on your chest or your belly and let it move as you breathe in and out several times.

Your body talks all the time, and breathing is one of its favourite languages. Fast breathing can mean stress, excitement. Slow breathing could mean relaxation, sleepiness, hypothermia. Breathing is in fact the oldest skill you have ever practiced. And controlling your breathing often controls the mind.

Tip and Practice, Swim 5

The Tip! Controlled breathing is a must-have skill of self-leadership. We start with breathing as an innate ability, and we turn it onto a skill.

The Practice! We are going to learn four patterns of breathing, and each pattern will create different sensations.

1. Breathe in through your nose and out through your nose, taking your time. This is our most usual pattern of breathing.
2. Breathe in through your mouth and out through your mouth. This pattern is often used when speaking, especially when speaking fast.
3. Breathe in through your nose and out through your mouth. This pattern is also often used when speaking, especially to calm down a nervous speaker.
4. Breathe in through your mouth and out through your nose. You may have had to think about it. If you had been swimming this pattern would have been your natural choice.

Repeat pattern 1 five times, then switch to pattern 2 five times, and so on. If you feel light-headed take a break or pause the pattern you were using for a moment. When ready extend the time you spend with each pattern.

Swim 6: Unique and yet the same

There is a paradox I particularly like, and it goes like this: unique and yet the same. We – as human beings – are all the same, with the same needs, same emotions, and yet this is what allows us to be so unique and different.

We are all driven by needs which are to be fulfilled. I am thinking here about Maslow's hierarchy of needs and its six levels[3]:

1. Physiological needs – like do I have enough to eat today,
2. Safety needs – am I safe to sleep somewhere this evening,
3. Social belonging – am I part of a group,
4. Self-esteem – can I recognise value in me, the individual,
5. Self-actualisation – am I reaching my full potential as an individual,
6. Self-transcendence – am I a spiritual being – part of the universe.

Each of us is driven by these six types of needs. How we decide to fulfil them, and how we experience them, are what make us unique and different.

Can you remember when you started developing this strong sense of being unique and different? You were about two years old. And you went through the famous "No-Phase", also labelled "The Terrible Twos".

What do we discover with this phase?

Several things. We are not an extension of our parents and the world around us. We are different than others. We can claim it – and saying "No" was our first way to express it. We could be part of the group, leave with others and still be different. Unique and yet the same.

Tip and Practice, Swim 6

The Tip! Applying self-leadership implies accepting, at the same time, to be different, and to be all the same. We are unique fishes, among many fishes, just like you and me. And it's okay.

The Practice! On a daily basis, observe how each of us has so many different ways to do something, from working to cooking to organising a house. Notice how this still allows us to stay connected with each other. Note when this even creates a stronger bond with a sense of complementarity.

Swim 7: We are all born explorers

One day you let your mouth open, breathing in quickly before making your first sound – and yes it was a big loud cry, and was probably painful. This was also your first breath of air; and it was worth the effort, right?

One day you decided to pull up on that table, stretching yourself to stand, engaging your ab muscles. This was your first attempt in standing, a pre-requisite before walking. It was intense and tough. You had to repeat it several times before it could give you walking, running, hiking, dancing, team sports, and many more; and it was worth the effort, right?

In fact, your highest achievements as an explorer and adventurer happened in the first six to seven years of your life, when every single day brought you something unknown to do. Every single day you had to step into the wild, and you did it. Some of us with boldness, others with shyness; still we all did it. And it was worth the effort, right?

These first six to seven years we even easily accepted that repeating an action was part of successfully learning a skill. We kept practising it again and again taking each repetition as an opportunity to improve. And we repeated the actions, widening our range of possibilities. Exploring.

Tip and Practice, Swim 7

The Tip! We are all born explorers. In fact, we all have an innate capability at exploring new activities and skills. At the same time we remember and relearn this, we are going to rediscover the ease and joy of putting an effort into something.

The Practice! First, identify some simple tasks. Then perform them in a different way than usual. For instance: rather than carrying your bag on one shoulder, carry it on your other shoulder; when locking your door, if you are to take your key in your left hand, take your key in your right hand; when coming home choose to follow a different route home; have fun eating while holding your fork with your non-dominant hand, etc.

Play with this Practice Swim 7, and notice how it is easy to feel strong when we successfully perform an action differently than usual.

Some extra swimming for the highly motivated

Feel like swimming further with some added practice? Enjoy!

Extra Practice on Swim 1, observation – We can describe observations as what we see, what we hear, what we smell, what we feel and what we taste. To observe is therefore about using our five primary senses. Each day take a moment to focus on one specific sense. For instance – when it is safe to do so, close your eyes and focus on everything you can hear – or close your eyes and focus on everything you can feel with your body, inside and outside your body. Now repeat the same exercise, keeping your eyes open this time, learning to focus one sense while still using the other four. Next, do that as you perform your normal daily tasks, learning to continuously observe. What are we looking for? The realisation of how much we can observe with our five primary senses in every single moment.

Extra Practice on Swim 5, breathing – With Swim 5, we identify four different patterns of breathing:

1. Breathe in through your nose and out through your nose.
2. Breathe in through your mouth and out through your mouth.
3. Breathe in through your nose and out through your mouth.
4. Breathe in through your mouth and out through your nose.

What other patterns of breathing do you already use?

As you go through your daily activities see which ones you can identify. If you run, for example, you would be using different patterns of breathing depending on your running speed. If you watch a suspense movie you may notice another breathing pattern coming into play when you hold your breath at times.

Note down as much as you can in your notebook. You may even start to notice how actively changing your breathing changes something in your mind. If you do, enjoy the discovery, because we will come back to that very soon.

A moment of reflection in the aquarium

Seven Swims completed; the habit of regular practice on the way, and our first step-back moment with three easy questions:

1) My Favourite Swims in this chapter

2) The Practice Swims I do everyday

3) The Swims for which I have no patience yet

2, Seven Myths to Unfold

I would rather have a mind opened by wonder than one closed by belief.

– Gerry Spence

Fish to fish

Here we are, enriched with seven useful observations – seven useful factual pieces of information and a definite fact: we do already have seven skills or tools of self-leadership. We may have forgotten we had them; we may be unsure on how to use them; and we are building up habits in using them.

What about unfolding and unwrapping seven myths now?

Myths are like beliefs we take for granted. They often define boxes within which we live happily and are full of confidence, circling in our aquariums.

What if these myths were just a specific perspective?

One lens in front of our eyes as we look through the window ...

The off-switch in the aquarium is still on. You apply your sense of autonomy and decide to extend the time period this off-switch remains activated. In this slow motion replay where you see every detail on the finish line, you wonder ... What if there was more than one finish line? What if there was more than one aquarium? And you see, once more, every single one of your moves; everything, from attitudes to perspectives and what makes the world around you.

Swim 8: The myth of knowing oneself

Seven in the morning and I am typing on my laptop. Do I need to know my laptop inside out to type sentences on the screen? Not really. I need partial information like – how to switch it on – how to check the battery level – how to open the right software. And I need to know what I want to do with my laptop.

Ten in the morning and as I leave my flat I lock the door. Do I need to know how the lock is built to lock the door? Not really. I need again partial knowledge like – what key to use – how to use it. And I need to know that I want to close the door.

I am now cycling to work. Do I need to know everything about the laws of physics to cycle? Not really. Partial knowledge here again is sufficient, assuming I know where I want to cycle.

Tell me then, when it comes to us human beings why are we so focussed on gathering *full knowledge*, aiming to know one's self inside out, rather than focusing on this simple question: "what do I want to see happen?"

Having a *partial knowledge* of who we are is very important. To do so, we observe. We collect information on our habits, our perceptions. We look for links between experiences and reactions. We monitor our reactions. However, to unfold this myth we want to move our focus from knowing oneself to knowing what we want to see happen, and embrace the idea, "It's okay to move on with partial information".

Tip and Practice, Swim 8

The Tip! Knowing oneself fully is overrated and partial knowledge is sufficient. Knowing what we want to see happen is much more useful.

The Practice! Focus on things you would like to see happen today. It could be something you'd like to say, something you'd like to see, or something you'd like to do. Note them down in your notebook. Once done, relax, observe and monitor how things go. You are likely to do these things quicker than you thought.

Swim 9: The myth of understanding

It is 1939 and Frida Khalo – an amazing Mexican artist – is exhibiting some of her paintings in Paris, the city of the French Surrealist movement. André Breton, a well-known surrealist, is enthusiastic, finding her art some of the most powerful surrealist paintings he has seen. To André's comments, Frida replied: 'They said I am a surrealist, but I am not. I've never painted dreams. I paint my reality.'

What happened there? When André Breton commented on Frida's art he did it from his perception and his perception at that time revolved around surrealism. He assumed he understood her while he was, in fact, giving an interpretation based on what he wanted to see.

The way we give meaning to our experiences is extremely subjective. The only way we may fully understand someone is to be in their head. Only then we would see everything exactly as they do, with all the background information collected since their birth; all their previous experiences, all their memories, etc. As such, understanding is like an optical illusion, created through the distorted lenses of our experiences, memories and feelings. And what we call understanding is no more than an interpretation.

To unfold this myth, we want to move our focus from ***understanding*** to ***acknowledging*** – shifting where we spend our energy from creating interpretation to using factual information. This could mean to collect information, to observe, to agree or not with an action, to accept a situation, to acknowledge how it impacts us, and to make a choice about it – as being okay with it or not, and so on.

Tip and Practice, Swim 9

The Tip! Understanding is like an optical illusion. A change of focus from understanding to acknowledging shifts where we spend our energy.

The Practice! Think about a situation or a person you have been focusing on understanding. Wipe out everything you know about the situation. And now look for factual information about this situation; collect every factual piece you can find. Once done, acknowledge each of the facts. It may mean to acknowledge how a fact impacts you; it may mean to make a choice on how to react in light of the fact, etc.

Swim 10: The myth of self-awareness

The word self-awareness is in fashion, but what is self-awareness?

- A good knowledge and judgement about oneself? (*cambridge.org*)
- A quality of being conscious of one's own feelings, characters, etc.? (*collinsdictionary.com*)
- A capacity for introspection and the ability to recognise oneself as an individual separate from the environment and other individuals? (*wikiepedia.org*)
- An awareness of one's own personality or individuality? (*merriam-webster.com*)

Have any of these definitions helped you? Probably not.

To undo the myth of self-awareness, let's apply partial knowledge and take self-awareness as being aware of the self, where the *self* is *me* or *my physical me*. Wherever you are, your physical me is surrounded with elements external to you. All of these elements form a system, and within it you are one element; more or less independent, more or less influenced, though always connected with the system. Being aware of the physical me becomes monitoring or acknowledging our interactions within the system **me-others-environment**.

The first step of self-awareness, therefore, is the monitoring of everything happening *outside the self*. The second step is the monitoring of everything happening *inside the self* in reaction to the system; the third step …

Tip and Practice, Swim 10

The Tip! Self-awareness is about monitoring the system me-others-environment. Practising self-awareness starts with observing and monitoring everything around us.

The Practice! You have now been practising observations daily. Observing is collecting factual information on the system me-others-environment. Let's add the next layer and see how these observations can impact how we interact with the system. Each day, when convenient, observe three things (factual information). Next, assess if the observations made (e.g. It's sunny outside; I received a bill in the post, etc.) change anything on your impression and/or sensation at that moment.

Swim 11: The myth of the fixed personality

The idea that our brain stops growing and evolving once we reach 20 years old, coupled with the belief that we stop producing neurons around 25 years old, has probably been one of the biggest myths of the past century. And yet, at the end of the 19th Century, William James – an American philosopher and psychologist – using facts and observations as evidence, already debated on the brain's capability for growth. However, we had to wait for the development of MRI and other brain imaging technologies to finally recognise the constant capability of our brain for evolving, changing, growing and repairing itself.

This brain capability is called Neuroplasticity, or brain plasticity. Norman Doidge, a neuroscientist researcher, actually coined the terms of "positive plasticity", such as recovering capabilities after a stroke, and "negative plasticity" which can be negative habits such as drug addiction, an obsessive-compulsive disorder or alcoholism.

How do we use this to unfold the myth of the fixed personality?

Your personality refers to how you apprehend life. You can be funny, extroverted, sporty, energetic, laid back, optimistic, etc. and this influences *how you think* and *how you do something*. However, the reverse is also true. Take the example of learning through imitating a role model. By modelling someone's behaviour we change how we do things and with repetition this creates a change in our brain and later in our personality.

Tip and Practice, Swim 11

The Tip! Personality can change. This is an extremely strong piece of knowledge of self-leadership. If there is something you do not like about your personality, you can change it.

The Practice! Modelling someone is *doing something as someone does*; for instance, modelling a gym instructor, a language teacher, a manager, modelling a really good friend, etc.

Think about someone you have been modelling recently. How has that changed how you do something? How long have you been doing it? What else have you noticed that has changed? Assess and note down in your notebook.

Swim 12: The myth of mind and body disconnection

When working on Swim 9, we left one question up in the air: what is the *self*. We won't answer that question today but let's bring one new brick onto that conversation.

It's the 17th century in our Western world, and a strong debate between philosophers makes it to the front page. The French Philosopher, Descartes, is strongly arguing against the Dutch Philosopher, Spinoza; until Descartes' famous *"Cogito Ergo Sum"* – "I think therefore I am" – finally wins the race. The self, hidden behind the sentence "I am" is voted a product of reason, where reason is the application of logic, theories, empirical evidence, etc. With the defeat of Spinoza, we not only lose the emotions, we also lose the assumption that humans are a complex mind-brain-body connected system.

Three centuries later in 1994, the myth of the mind and body disconnection finally unfolds, and the famous *"Cogito Ergo Sum"* makes it back to the front page, slightly rewritten: "I feel therefore I am". With his book, *Descartes' Error,* Antonio Damasio argues: "The division between reason and passion, or cognition and emotion (an opposition that goes all the way back to Aristotle) is, from a neurological point of view, a fallacy." Thanks to IRM and other methodologies, we can show a decision is as much driven by emotions as thought; and people with a specific type of brain damage (where areas processing emotions are impacted), are unable to make suitable decisions. Therefore, we can no longer fully separate the brain and the mind.

Tip and Practice, Swim 12

The Tip! Mind and body are two sides of the same coin; always in interaction with each other, and influencing each other. Changing something in how you use your body can actually change your mind.

The Practice! Let's play with this modified sentence: "I take a body pose therefore I am …" For example, "I stand on my two feet like a tree; therefore I am as strong as a tree". For ideas on poses to use watch Amy Cuddy[4] Ted Talk. Always maintain the chosen body pose for two minutes. Then note any useful observations in your notebook; making sure you are focusing on factual information.

Swim 13: The myth of confidence

Confidence is a tricky word; one of these easily confused abstract words. First, it is linked to two separate meanings; one implying strength and certitude, i.e. having confidence, while the other meaning in secret and hiding, i.e. in confidence. Also, it is often defined by even more abstract words, such as feeling, belief, or faith.

One definition is: confidence is "the feeling or belief that one can have faith in or rely on someone or something." Another definition gives: "confidence is about one's ability to succeed." This last definition is simpler, so let's apply it to a life situation.

Let's say I am worried about doing something – in my head I even see myself not doing it. I am therefore confident in my ability to succeed at not being able to do it. If instead I do see myself doing it – even though being worried about it – I become confident in my ability in doing it. This is excellent, right? Whatever the situation and the result, I am therefore confident.

What if we all have confidence? What if the problem is actually about the skill or situation onto which we choose to apply our confidence? Unfolding the myth of confidence therefore means to put our focus on skills and situations.

Tip and Practice, Swim 13

The Tip! You have confidence. Until today you may just have applied it to the wrong skill, situation, objective or goal.

The Practice! Identify a situation –A– where you came with the confidence of not being able to do something and ended up not being able to do it. Then identify other situations –B– where even if you had this negative impression of not being able to do something, you did manage to complete the task or activities. Compare the factual information you listed for situations A and B. What important factual information is present in situation B which may be missing in situation A? What helped you to focus on the right output for situation B?

With this practice we explore the paradigm of self-fulfilling prophecies, and as a self-leader we want our prophecies to help us.

Swim 14: The myth of people not liking change

Some time ago I came across these two great quotes. The first from W. Edwards Deming, an economist from the 20th century: "It is not necessary to change. Survival is not mandatory." And the second from Heraclitus, a Greek philosopher from way back in the history of time, centuries and centuries ago, "Change is the only constant."

It's a fact, either in life or in business, change is the only constant and yet, there is that myth in the world: 'People do not like to change.' If that was true, couples would never get kids and the human race would definitely not exist! Life is simply built around change.

It's not change that people don't like, it's not having the ownership or the control of that change – and the impact associated with it.

A 2014 movie, "Two Days, One Night", gives a perfect example of this. Sandra, the main character, discovers on a Friday evening that her co-workers have opted for a significant pay bonus leading to her dismissal. On hearing the news, she retreats into a state of passivity and panic. However her husband and two of her friends motivate her to take action: to visit each of her co-workers and ask them to review their decision. The following Monday morning, even though enough of her co-workers agreed to support her, and the management team review their decision, Sandra refuses to keep her job. After all her effort and her success at keeping her job, she refuses it; calm, determined, strong and very clear headed, and creates the change she initially feared.

To unfold the myth of change we want to focus on getting back ownership of changes around us.

Tip and Practice, Swim 14

__The Tip!__ People like to change when they have ownership of the change. If you are not happy with a change, ask yourself "How can I recover ownership of either the change or the situation?"

__The Practice!__ Starting today, pay attention to changes you create every day, such as: changing a restaurant, changing a haircut, etc. At the same time, pay attention to changes you experience though do not choose. If any annoyed you, note them down in your notebook.

Some extra swimming for the highly motivated

Feel like swimming further with some added practice? Enjoy!

Extra Practice on Swim 10, the myth of self-awareness – We often link the self to a sense of identity. Some of us are really good at spontaneously associating "I am ..." with a follow up statement, for instance:

I am   <Your name>, tall, small, sporty, nervous, calm, etc.

Even if you do not like writing a sentence starting with "I am", for the purpose of your evolution with this chapter have a go at it.

Once you have a few sentences written, pause, and then see how you can rewrite them with something like "I do the process of ..." or "I go through the process of ..."

Now reverse the sentence. Imitating Descartes and the famous "I think therefore I am", for instance "I play the piano therefore I am ..." etc.

Take a moment to take on board all the many variations you have already listed on this idea of self.

Extra Practice on Swim 13, the myth of confidence – Let's look at the word "confidence". What does it mean to you? An easy way to find this out is to transform it into a "conscious word" in 3 easy steps.

1. Write CONFIDENCE vertically on your page, one letter per line.
2. For each letter find a word, a noun or an adjective, that you want to associate with confidence. You can do it for specific contexts e.g. a meeting, a driving lesson, or you can do it for all situations.
3. Where possible turn it into a sentence (optional).

A very famous sample on the internet of a "conscious word" is *FAIL*, as

F   *First*
A   *Attempt*
I   *In*
L   *Learning*

Another example with *OPTIMISM*, gives us "*Ongoing Permission To Inspire Many Individuals in being Self-motivated.*"

A moment of reflection in the aquarium

Unfolding myths means swimming outside our aquarium. Keep up the regular practice and enjoy our second step-back moment with our three questions:

1) My Favourite Swims in this chapter

2) The Swims Practice I do everyday

3) The Swims for which I am struggling to let go

3, Seven Habits in Your Survival Kit

Simplicity is the ultimate sophistication.

– Leonardo da Vinci

Fish to fish

First, we explored seven useful observations. Then we unfolded seven myths.

What about taking the time to establish not only a foundation, but a very practical survival kit with seven strong habits? Seven strong habits – which are as much habits as tools – we can use easily in any situation, especially challenging ones.

Why that notion of challenging situations?

What is a challenging situation?

Why would we want to be able to apply self-leadership effectively in challenging situations?

Challenging situations are any situations which challenge us. And usually we struggle to manage or handle them. Challenging situations are a good test to our self-leadership. The more self-leadership you show, the more calm and composed you remain through any type of situation. Rather than controlling the situations, you'll focus in controlling your reactions.

What do we need in our survival kit then?

Seven actions: easy to remember and apply. Seven tools: perfect to use to get us out of trouble. Seven habits: to turn into daily "feeling good" habits.

With this survival kit we are working on our self-leader foundation state of mind; that is a default state of mind we can easily go to in which we can always express our self-leadership. You want to see that foundation as the starting point of the spiral of growth we talked about in the introduction. From that central point we are going to layer skills and competencies in self-leadership, expanding the spiral as we go along.

It is time now. Time to release that switch in the aquarium.

The water is going to flow a lot faster, and you're ready. You have an anchor – your body – and seven habits coming soon; like the strong muscles you need to swim anywhere you want.

Swim 15: Breathe and drink

Have you noticed how fishes cannot go without water? They actually breathe through it. We are not ready to do the same yet, but we are ready to always keep in mind two things:

- TO DRINK WATER regularly, especially when we feel a drop in energy, or we feel our mind is slowing down.
- TO BREATHE in and out regularly and slowly, especially when we feel an unwanted change of rhythm in our breathing, or an unpleasant acceleration. When that happens focus for a few seconds on counting even periods of breathing in and out, over 3s, then 4s, then 5s, until you reach 6s.

What comes first? The breath you take which gives you time to drink water? Or the drink of water you take which forces you to pause and breathe. Whichever wins the race, two things happen:

1. The provision of oxygen (either as oxygen or as water). And without either water or oxygen, our body cannot function. For instance, about 60% of the human body is actual water, located mainly in the brain, heart, kidneys, bones and blood. Then our cells use oxygen to break down sugar to produce most of the energy we need to function normally.
2. The creation of a gesture, e.g. the movement of hands or arms. And this acts as a pattern interrupt, breaking the flow of whatever could be challenging us.

Tip and Practice, Swim 15:

The Tip! Drink water regularly, ideally without waiting to be thirsty, and never too much at once. Breathe in a regular rhythm. When possible breathe in and out over the same number of seconds.

The Practice! For the next 3 or 4 days, firstly monitor how much water you drink – not alcohol, tea or coffee, but water. Pay particular attention to drinking water during meetings, especially long meetings. Secondly, identify your natural rhythm of breathing in and out. When you're at rest observe your breathing pattern. Is it shallow? Is it even – breathing in as long as breathing out? Is your belly moving? Are your shoulders rising? Is it hurried? As usual write these facts in your notebook.

Swim 16: Develop a default posture

Our body, with its physical presence, is an anchor for our mind (Swim 4); an anchor rooting us in the moment. With this swim 16 today, we want to make this anchor a safe place, and a source of energy and strength. Developing physical stability and strength of the body can then be communicated to the mind. We are going to develop a default "grounding" posture with 5 easy steps to follow:

1. Stand your two feet hip-width apart on the ground.
2. Effortlessly breathe in and breathe out.
3. Let your arms hang loosely down alongside the body, chest up from the stomach and relax as you let go of any tension.
4. Breathe in a bit stronger and wider, and visualise something which means stability for you. It can be a tree; your feet like roots into the ground. It can be a heavy rock. It can be a house; your feet the very strong foundations. Just choose something you associate with stability.
5. Engage all your muscles in a smooth equilibrium, thinking firmness free of tension. Shoulders are free of tension. Chest is up from the stomach. And your focus locked onto easiness and firmness.

With this default posture, you are creating a default way of standing, which you can go back to easily and effortlessly any time as appropriate.

Tip and Practice, Swim 16:

The Tip! A great grounding posture is a dynamic posture, feet hip-width apart, arms down alongside the body, chest up, muscles firm and relaxed engaged in a smooth equilibrium.

The Practice! Every day practice the 5-step sequence above. Give it a name, like "My default state", "My ground state" or "My tree state", so you can easily associate the name with the 5-step sequence. When saying its name it should bring you automatically into it. Start practising going into your default posture any time you want during the day – in meetings, on public transportation, etc.

If standing is not easy for you, develop this posture sitting. Use the chair or the ground your feet are resting on to anchor your body. As suggested while standing, look for a sitting position that is firm, dynamic, still relaxed.

Swim 17: Maintain awareness

Wherever we are we are surrounded with elements external to us. All of these elements form a system. In fact, we are just one other element within this system; more or less independent, more or less influenced, and always fully connected with the system. Self-awareness is about monitoring how we interact with this *me-others-environment*, and a key to self-awareness and to this ongoing monitoring is an extremely great sense of observation. Maintaining awareness is about maintaining this continuous observation of everything around us, and thus continuous monitoring on how we interact with it or react to it.

What is so important about maintaining awareness?

Everything we observe is an actual event which we record through our senses and then process through our database of experience. These events are factual information. They can act as stimuli and trigger specific moods, mental states, actions, etc. And they can act as solutions; factual information to use in order to change the interactions within the system. The more accurate we are about everything happening in the system, the more choices we will have to influence the system. And we explore this in depth with our next chapters.

Tip and Practice, Swim 17:

The Tip! Maintaining awareness is maintaining a continuous observation of everything happening in the system me-others-environment. And the more accurate we are about everything happening around us, the more options in our reactions we can choose from.

The Practice! In Swim 1, we practiced observations with our five senses. In Swim 10, we linked observations with our impressions of the moment. With this Swim, we are adding the next layer: developing a complete commitment to observation. Wherever you are, whatever you do, make an effort to tune your mind, body, and five senses to everything around you. Notice people moving. Notice what time it is. Notice what the weather is. Still do your tasks and at the same time notice what furniture is around you. Notice if anything changed in your colleague's facial expressions. Notice what sounds you can hear. Train your mind and body to observe every single thing there is to observe, while still doing your daily activities.

Swim 18: Stay relaxed

If you search the internet on the expression ***staying relaxed***, you may be surprised not to find anything on *staying relaxed* but instead information on *staying calm and cool*. However, calm and relaxed are two very different things. If I run a half-marathon I need to stay relaxed in order to run as long as possible, and here I may have a focus on muscle relaxation. If I go horse riding I also want to stay relaxed in order to follow the movement of the horse; here again I will be looking for the muscle relaxation. If I attend a training course, I will also focus on staying relaxed in order to keep an open mind, and because I know relaxation helps the memory process. However, calm and cool may not be a good idea; excitement and curiosity may be more helpful.

What do we mean by *staying relaxed*, therefore?

We are looking at relaxation as the opposite of tension. And by staying relaxed, we look at developing a sense of things being fluid and keeping up with the flow, with minimal expenditure of physical, mental and emotional energy.

"To develop a sense" is subjective; an actual impression and, to give us maximum chances to achieve this impression, we are going to focus on using factual information – precisely biofeedback, such as heartbeat and muscle tension. We get this information with two simple questions:

1. Are my muscles soft and relaxed, dynamic and free of unnecessary tension?   Yes/No
2. Is my heartbeat regular?   Yes/No

And of course when an answer is "No", we then go through a set of actions, and repeat it until we can answer "Yes".

How do we do that then – *staying relaxed*?

We start with muscles. Keeping a muscle soft and relaxed may not be that straight forward, but identifying tension can be easier. Take your hand and close your fist very tight, so tight that you feel the muscle tensing up to your shoulder. Your forearm may even start to shake as you do so. And now open your fist, releasing the tension. Your arm will immediately relax. Forcing a tension, then releasing it, immediately brings relaxation, and this is our first step.

What about our heartbeat now?

When it comes to the heart, we find quite a few things of interest. The heart, independently of culture, religion, countries, is an important symbol associated with many metaphors. At the same time, the heart is a very simple muscle – a strong one but still only a muscle. Recent research shows the heart can send a message to the brain, as if the heart knows before the brain (see the HeartMath Institute in the USA[5]); and we can find evidence of a *heart brain*. Also the heart has a beat, and this beat creates a rhythm – a wave pattern – which can change. This rhythm is called Heart Rate Variability (or HRV). When we get excited or nervous, the beat accelerates; when we sleep a good resting sleep, the beat slows down.

Something that may seem obvious: your heart rate is actually linked to your breathing rate. If you like being technical, this phenomenon is called "respiratory sinus arrhythmia (RSA)". As you normally breathe in, your heart rate increases slightly and then, as you breathe out, it decreases[6]. This means that having a very regular breathing rhythm will influence your heart rhythm (or HRV). To stay relaxed, we are going to focus on using a very regular pattern of breathing in and out, and develop what we call a coherent HRV. This is our second step.

Tip and Practice, Swim 18:

The Tip! To stay relaxed we focus on two things: keeping our muscles free of tension, and breathing in and out regularly and slowly. And we can do that at the same time or in any order we want.

The Practice! Step 1. Sit comfortably. Focusing on breathing in and out through your nose, inhale for four seconds then exhale for four seconds. Repeat for two minutes. If easier, directly inhale for five or six seconds then exhale for the same length of time period of five or six seconds. When starting with four seconds, practice this rhythm gradually increasing to five seconds until you are able to reach an even period of six seconds. Next, repeat this while walking, driving, cycling, etc.

Step 2. Again sit comfortably. Focusing on your eyes; close them as tightly as you can, then release. Focusing on your belly; pull your belly button in as much as you can, then release. Repeat with other sets of muscles, like your arms, hands, etc. Next, repeat while doing an activity.

Swim 19: Acknowledge your emotions

It's 1872 and Charles Darwin published *The Expression of the Emotions in Man and Animal*. With his book he presents two arguments – 1. Human emotions link mental states with bodily movement. 2. Human emotions are genetically determined, deriving from purposeful animal actions. He even assumed through his writings that animals can experience emotions. This last thought was truly scandalous at that time: emotions were only associated with humans and emotions were understood as learned behaviours, only existing in some cultures or societies. About a century later, thanks to the work of Dr. Paul Ekman and his lab, we have a very different picture, and we now accept that there are six "universal emotions" – anger, disgust, fear, sadness, surprise, joy – universally recognisable in facial expressions.

Nowadays, emotions are in fashion. A full branch in history is studying the history of emotions, a complex subject burdened by cultures and languages (see Tiffany Watt and her TED talk, *The History of Human Emotions[7]*). Neuroscientists are getting involved as well; we have already discussed some of the work of the neuroscientist, Antonio Damasio, with our Swim 4, and the unfolding of the myth of mind and body disconnection. Even now emotional intelligence is taught in business school.

What actually is an emotion?

The word itself comes from the Latin *ex (e)* for out, and *movere* for move. An emotion is something which moves us out into an action. Let's use this through our practice as our first way to acknowledge emotions.

Tip and Practice, Swim 19:

The Tip! Emotions move us into actions. Acknowledging emotions starts with acknowledging what moves us into action.

The Practice! Before the end of your day sit and pause. Then look at the actions you took during the day. What moved you into those actions? Were there any actions that were easier to do? Now think about what you want to do tomorrow. What makes you put these actions on the agenda? Think about planning your next vacation. What pops up in your mind when you start the planning? Finish by listing in your notebook all the emotions you are familiar with – if any.

Swim 20: Maintain movement

Have you noticed how everything is based on movement?

Not convinced? Ask your beating heart then. When it stops moving, which is called a heart attack, everything else stops with it; your life too.

We have a heart and it always moves with its regular rhythm. We have blood flowing through veins and arteries. We have hormones and other clever sets of chemicals always in movement, continuously changing and maintaining equilibrium. We have bones and skin and although they look solid, they are made of moving elements such as atoms.

An object like a window, which appears immobile, is an element in permanent movement, a movement so slow our eyes find it impossible to detect. Our worlds – plural to represent all our different cultures, societies, urban or countries landscapes – are in continuous movement; be it either wind rustling through leaves in a park, or a flow of cars and bicycles along a street.

Your voice, when you talked to a friend, creates movement; an actual acoustic wave which can be recorded through the movement it generates in objects close-by.[8]

What if movement was a tool? What if creating movement was a way to maintain ownership of a situation? What if maintaining movement was a skill of self-leadership?

Tip and Practice, Swim 20:

The Tip! Everything is based on movement, and movement is everywhere. As part of developing self-leadership, we are going to develop a habit of maintaining and encouraging movement.

The Practice! To start, we are going to focus on the creation of physical movement. In the next few days, notice each time you create a physical movement. Notice how you do it. Notice how your mind reacts when you focus on the physical movement. Next, practice your "default posture" from Swim 16. Notice how this default posture relies on small movements to keep stability and strength. As you remain immobile notice how each muscle actually performs a mini movement.

Swim 21: Partner up

There is often more behind the scene that what we see.

When, on August 31st 2013, Diana Nyad entered the water to start a 100 mile swim (which is now a world record), a team of 35 people was supporting her, working behind the scenes and invaluable to the accomplishment. When Mike Horn set to walk through the South Pole by himself, a much more limited team was there, but still there was a team which supported him way before he started his walk.

Knowing how to get support is, in fact, an amazing skill. Our first step in developing this skill is going to acknowledge a key partner we often take for granted. This partner is a special person, someone that has been with us every single moment of our lives; the bad ones and the good ones. We do not always agree with this person, still we need to recognise this person has always been by our side. If you have not worked out whom I am talking about, take a few steps toward a mirror and look into it.

Yes. Us. Our own self has always been with us, every single day of our life, and it's time to acknowledge it. It's actually time to partner up.

This starts by forgetting about sentences such as 'Fight with yourself', 'In the room, the only enemy is you', 'You have only one person to beat, and it's you'. Why? A straight-forward fact: when there is a winner, there is always a loser. Whatever way you look at it, as soon as you win over yourself, you also lose. Indeed a part of you loses.

Hence the importance to partner-up, that every aspect of our self can win.

Tip and Practice, Swim 21:

The Tip! Even though you may not see it yet, you have always been here for yourself, every single day of your life. So it's time to learn how to partner up. Time to become one of your best partners.

The Practice! To become our best partner can be slightly disconcerting. Let's start simple. Every day listen to the words you use, either when talking about yourself or when talking to yourself. Scribble them down in your notebook. Pay attention to any recurring wording or expressions.

Some extra swimming for the highly motivated

Feel like swimming further with some added practice? Enjoy!

Extra Practice on Swim 15, with breathing and body connection –
With our Swim 5, we practiced four patterns of breathing, focusing on
how we inhale and exhale, using either our mouth or our nose. We are
now going to focus on breathing and body connection. First, place a
hand on your chest and the other on your belly:

- As you breathe in focus on pushing your belly against your hands so
  that your hands move with the rhythm you create. Your hand on your
  chest should remain in place. Count how long you breathe in.
- Now, keep the hand on your belly fixed in place, and this time focus on
  moving your chest against your other hand, moving this hand up and
  down. It is likely the rhythm is shorter with a smaller intake of breath.
  Count how long you breathe in and see if you can do the same as
  before when breathing into your belly. You may sense your back
  muscles responding as your ribcage opens more.
- Lastly, get both hands moving. Start with the belly hand and then the
  chest hand. Repeat this a few times, creating a wave movement, then
  switch; your chest hand first and the belly hand next.

When we practice breathing exercises, we practice *controlled breathing* or
controlling our breathing to create a change in physiology.

Extra Practice on Swim 16, the default posture – First go into your
default posture using the 5-step sequence from Swim 16. Stand your
two feet on the ground, hip-width apart, your arms hanging loosely
alongside the body, chest up and relax. Then:

- Explore moving your body weight to the front of your toes, then to the
  back of your heels. Notice which muscle goes into action to keep the
  balance depending on the body weight location. Bring your weight
  back to the middle above your hips and the soles of your feet.
- Focus on the feeling of being in-balance as you stay standing, relaxed
  and dynamic. What image came to mind? Write this information down
  in your notebook. Document every detail which came into your mind
  as precisely as you can.

A moment of reflection in the aquarium

Seven more swims completed, and not just any type of swims, the seven swims of our survival and first aid kit. Let's have a moment of reflection with three easy questions:

1) What are the seven Swims of your survival kit?

2) What are the Practice Swims I do every day?

3) What are the Swims I'd like to know more about?

Congratulations!

You've reached self-leadership level 1

You know you have innate ability in self-leadership
You have unpacked seven myths giving you more ability in self-leadership
You have your survival kit, and with it seven habits of self-leadership

4, Seven Perspectives to the Self

We don't see things as they are; we see them as we are.

– Anais Nin

Fish to fish

Let's go back to our definition of self-leadership.

Self-leadership is having a developed sense of who we are, what we can do and where we are going, coupled with the ability to influence our communication, emotions and behaviours along the way.

A long sentence packed with information and potential. There are a few starting points to explore, such as *who we are*, *what we can do*, *where we are going*. Then we have this word *ability* which means we should be able to link self-leadership to the development of skills and competencies. And lastly we introduce the idea that everything will go through *communication, emotions and behaviours*; that to be able to go where we want we only need to be able to influence these three.

The seven habits of our survival kit are the first tools we have to influence our emotions and behaviours. When you want to influence something or someone firstly you would usually identify what you want to influence them about. With our survival kit, we have a very clear focus; *keeping our cool* – hence the practice on breathing and on staying relaxed. By keeping our cool, we are actually in the practice of avoiding automatic reactions, giving us the opportunity to step back and choose how to react to a situation. We speak about using *critical thinking* versus *automatic reactions*.

This is how we influence our behaviours, by stepping back and choosing how to react. And we can already do that with our survival kit. Now we want to strengthen this capability. For this to happen, we need to better comprehend the aquarium we are living in, especially how we interact with the system me-others-environment (Swim 10).

Now, when it comes to systems, we can find a very interesting piece of knowledge within the field of cybernetics called the Ashby's Law or "the Law of requisite variety"; and it says:

"The variable within a system, with the most flexible behaviour, will control the system internal state, which should be kept as close as possible to the goal state".

Let's translate this sentence into our world. As human beings we are one variable within the system me-others-environment. And somehow we need to control this system. In the least we want this system to help us in going *where we want to go* which we could say is the goal state. To influence the system me-others-environment we therefore need to be the variable with the most flexible behaviour.

Wow! Neat, right!

Therefore, a strength of self-leadership is to develop flexibility. Of course, we need to have a better idea on what types of flexibility we have available, or what type of variable we truly are.

What about exploring seven perspectives to the idea of the self?

We could see these as seven perspectives on how we build this notion of self. And with that, we are going to explore the fact behind the self.

Now this is a complex subject. I would see the self as something dynamic, neither white nor black, more like a system in itself. A system within a system, and always in movement.

Maybe the self is a bit like a river. When you look at a river from a bridge you see one river. And this river has a name, a bed and a path. At the same time you know the water underneath you right now is not exactly the same as it was 5 or 10 minutes ago; and it is not the same that it will be in 10 or 15 minutes. It is no longer exactly the same river; even though it is the same river.

Welcome to the world of the self.

Swim 22: The self and the experiences

How do we experience the world around us?

How do we make sense of it?

They seem to be the same question but they're not. The first one is about the experience; the actual information about what has happened. The second one is about the interpretation; the personalised version of the experiences.

If you were to describe the experience you are currently having by describing the room you are in you are likely to start with what you see, hear, smell, feel and maybe taste. You will use information collected with your five senses[9]. At any single moment your senses are receiving a huge amount of information. The estimation is around 11 million pieces of information per second[10]. 11 million! And of all these, we are only going to process about 0.1% in an active way! 0.1%[11]! Our brain is specifically built to do this massive selection using filtering processes, such as deletion, distortion, and generalisation, keeping available only the 0.1% it thinks fit.

Since we experience the world through the information we record and analyse, what we experience is only a sub-set of the real experience built using partial information. But, how do we know this particular partial information is what we need? To answer this question, we need first to recover the missing information. We do that by undoing our filtering process, and it starts with the collection of factual information (facts). It starts with observations.

Tip and Practice, Swim 22:

The Tip! The recording of our experiences is based on partial and filtered or distorted information. Applying self-leadership requires us to recover the missing information and to revisit the content of our experiences.

The Practice! Discover the game of "Comparing Experiences". Organise a dinner, either with friends or family. At this dinner bring up something you all did together. Ask each person to recall their version of the event. Note how different each memory is. Note how each person focusses on something else. Does it tell you anything about that person?

Swim 23: The self and the facts

In the stories we build around us, facts and interpretations are two different sides of the same coin. Facts are owned by the ***experiential self*** – the *me* who goes through the experience; while interpretations are owned by the ***remembering self***[12] – the *me* who keeps memories. When we let the *remembering self* take over, we may disconnect ourselves from the facts; mislabelling experiences and, at times, turning interpretation into facts.

So how do we reconnect the *experiential self* and the facts?

First, we pause. To recover missing information, we have to first stop the automatic filtering done by our brain and we have to undo it too.

Second, once our brain is on pause we give it a direct task: we have to tell it to search for factual and unexpected. Only then can we bypass the automatic filtering. Somehow we have to prove to our own brain that there is more to the situation than what it is expecting.

What tools do we use?

Observation, observation and observation. And now we also add active questioning, using questions such as "What I am not seeing that I should see?", "Is there more to see than what I have already seen?" etc.

Tip and Practice, Swim 23:

The Tip! Facts and interpretations are two sides of the same coin. Take a moment to separate them. To get visibility on a complete situation always come back to the facts.

The Practice! Are your *experiential self* and *remembering self* talking the same language? Is your *remembering self* taking over at times? Let's find out. Every day for the next seven days, in as many situations as possible, put extra focus on your *experiential self*. Observe very carefully with your five senses. If in a challenging situation, focus on collecting only factual information happening in the moment. When assessing a situation, **s l o w   i t   d o w n** on purpose, and before making any comment **c h e c k** all base information is factual. At the end of the seven days, note how your week went. Was it a good week? Here again only use factual information to create that report.

Swim 24: The self and the actions

"Because we simply cheated ourselves a whole way down the line. We thought of life by analogy with a journey with a pilgrimage which had a serious purpose at the end; the thing was to get to that end, success or whatever it is. But we missed the point the whole way along it was a musical thing and you were supposed to sing or dance while the music was being" – Allan Watts[13]

Life is a music hall. Such an amazing metaphor. A music hall where stories interact with each other; where actors, sing, dance, jump, or rest on benches. We are actors. We all have something to act about. What if who we are – our self – was linked to what we can do, or what we want to do?

For those of you who may not have done your extra practice from page 41 on Swim 10, it's time to act. Step 1: write a sentence starting with "I am". Step 2: rewrite each sentence turning them into actions. For instance:

"I am a speaker"	becomes	"I practice public speaking"
	Or	"I do the process of public speaking"
"I am an aunt"	becomes	"I take the time to spend time with nieces and/or nephews"
"I am logical"	becomes	"I process information in a logical way"
"I am exuberant"	becomes	"I can process experiences in an exuberant way"

What are we doing here? From something vague linked to an idea of identity – "I am ..." – we extract precise information, giving us direction to act upon. Not only do we recover missing information, we now have either skills to improve or tasks to do.

Tip and Practice, Swim 24:

The Tip! Most of the time, "I am XYZ" can be rewritten with sentences such as "I (can) do the process of XYZ" or "I XYZ". We move our focus from identity to capability hence identify either skills to improve or tasks to do. We can now grow and develop.

The Practice! Easy: Complete steps 1 and 2 above. Do it slowly and meticulously. Next: Go back to your notes from practice Swim 21. When possible rewrite any of the noted sentences using step 2 above.

Swim 25: The self and the mood

Sunday morning ten o'clock; as you hear your alarm clock you turn, stretch like a cat, yawn then sit up – maybe with a smile on your face. As your feet are reaching for the ground and you stand, you are in a certain mood.

Monday morning six o'clock; as you hear your alarm clock you turn, stretch like a cat, yawn then sit up. As your feet are reaching for the ground and you stand, you are in a certain mood; and it is likely this mood is different than the one from the day before.

In psychology a mood is defined as an emotional state, however, not in a very specific way. It seems a mood combines a mix of psychological and emotional states at a certain time. It means a mood can vary through the days or depending on context. As a person we may feel we have a dominant mood; still this dominant mood will fluctuate with our daily activities and experiences. While on vacation our mood tends to be relaxed. When going through a rough time our mood may become gloomy. If we are sick our mood changes again, impacted by the health of our body. When in extremely good health the strength in our body brings strength to our mood; similarly being in a good mood makes us stronger in health. For me, moods are very closely related to *states of mind*.

What if I could influence this mood? What if I could even choose my mood? I can see how this would impact my actions. We are going to do that by first learning about *states of mind*.

Tip and Practice, Swim 25:

The Tip! Every single moment we are in a specific mood. This mood is created by a *state of mind*, and this state of mind affects how we experience situations. By influencing our state of mind we influence how we experience our day-to-day life, and later our actions.

The Practice! The first step is to get acquainted with our natural or spontaneous state of mind. As you go through your day pay attention to your mood. Notice which mood you are in in the morning. Notice which mood you are in at work. Notice which mood you are in in the evening. Pay attention when your mood is changing. If it changes, assess what has changed at the same time (look for factual information). Write in your notebook the identified mood and give it a name.

Swim 26: The self and the physiology

It's amazing to think that we are only a collection of neural processes.

We have a body and this body moves thanks to muscles which are activated by signals sent through neurons. We have a brain and this brain also activates thanks to signals sent through neurons. Take a memory. We see a memory as a picture in our brain. But for our brain to show us this picture, it has to fire a set of electrochemical signals in a very precise way; it has to resend the picture every single time. The brain is the post office, and the neurons, the courier agent.

A typical neuron, also called a nerve cell, consists of a soma, dendrites and an axon. A neuron receives, processes, and transmits information through electrical and chemical signals. The act of sending that message is called the neural (or neuronal) process. Neurons are the courier agent, specialising in delivering messages as quickly as possible. For that, they use chemical agents called hormones, like adrenaline, cortisol, oxytocin, dopamine, etc.

A few minutes with a pen in your mouth forces your face muscles into a genuine smile and your body generates oxytocin[14]. This hormone then travels through the blood stream, and the full physiology of your body changes. Soon, your mind no longer knows the difference between the real and the fake and you start to smile genuinely. A change in your body creates a change in your physiology and then in your state of mind.

Tip and Practice, Swim 26:

The Tip! Everything we do is possible thanks to neural processes, which combine electric and physiological processes. Our physiology can therefore influence our actions.

The Practice! When we apply our survival kit we are actually using our body to change our physiology, by using our default posture, or practicing controlled breathing. Let's explore this further. Let's observe how food and state of mind are connected. What happens when you lack food? What happens when you eat too much? What happens when you stop eating sugar for two or three days? Observe and note down the changes you feel. If you can, focus on sugar and extend the sugar free period for seven days.

Swim 27: The self and the idea of congruency

The word ***congruence*** comes from the Latin word *congruentia*, which stands for agreement, harmony, coming together. When we apply this to human beings we talk about congruency at the level of the person, and a person is acting in a congruent way when all actions, emotions, states of mind or thoughts focus in a similar direction. It is then as if everything in someone's world becomes consistent and wrapped all together. It does actually feel as if everything is ***coming together***.

So what does it mean to act in a congruent way?

Ask people going through the process of depression, what music they would like to listen to in order to feel better. They will reply – "happy", "lively", "cheerful". But then ask them to go and pick a track to listen to. They will choose sad pieces of music. In their current state of mind, which is gloomy, choosing happy music is close to impossible, and choosing sad music is the only congruent act they can think of. To choose a cheerful song while in their depressed state of mind, they would have to accept to be non-congruent, that is to choose an action not matching their thoughts.

Being congruent is good when it helps and widens our choices. When it does not, we have to learn to accept to not being congruent, and opening ourselves to choices "outside of our boxes". We have to accept discrepancy in our thought, and be okay with this mental disturbance. And yes, this is self-leadership.

Tip and Practice, Swim 27:

The Tip! Congruency is the idea of everything coming together. We talk about congruency (or cognitive consonance) versus non-congruency (or cognitive dissonance). Paying attention to conflicting information we tell ourselves helps in identifying possible congruency issues.

The Practice! Pay attention to your mood, i.e state of mind. At the same time listen to your self-talk, i.e. how you talk to yourself. Lastly take notes of your actions and identify the signs of congruency (or not)?

And next time you are looking for something missing, pay attention to what you are saying in your head. Then replace it with "I can find the missing item now." See how it makes a difference.

Swim 28: The self and the behaviours

We have all done it; decided to do something and then regretted it. Even just a few minutes or hours after making the decision, we could see it was not the best choice. And we often start moaning, name calling ourselves – "you did that again", "you idiot", "it's like you're doing it on purpose" etc.

What if we were actually doing it on purpose? What if we had a good reason to make this decision and choose this behaviour?

I'm sure you've heard about survival instinct. People and researchers remain amazed how we can surpass ourselves; exceeding limits in the name of *survival*. With such a strong survival instinct why would we ever choose to do something without our best interests at heart? With such a strong survival instinct how could we choose behaviours without being convinced this behaviour has a positive intention for us?

A very trivial example: you are asked to speak in public, and even though you like the idea, and you know it's good for your career or business, you shy away and say no. Of course you're not happy with your decision. Still you took it, and you probably took it to protect yourself, to avoid facing stage fright, etc. How do you find the exact positive intention in this decision? Simply ask, "What is the positive intention of saying no?" "What is the positive intention of having decided to do that?"

This is extremely powerful. When we know the positive intention behind our behaviours, we can partner up with ourselves (Swim 21) to identify a better behaviour to achieve the same positive intention.

Tip and Practice, Swim 28:

The Tip! Every single one of our behaviours has a positive intention – a positive intention for us, the fish swimming in the aquarium.

The Practice! Daily, for at least 7 days, identify the positive intention behind your actions or behaviour? Ask yourself this simple question: "What is the positive intention for me behind this behaviour?" Repeat this question until your answer:

1. Includes "I" as the subject;
2. is written in the present tense and;
3. is an affirmative sentence.

Some extra swimming for the highly motivated

Feel like swimming further with some added practice? Enjoy!

Extra Practice on our Swim 22, the self and the experience – Let's go back to this notion of being *the boss*. It may feel like an odd concept and it may surprise you just now, however it does happen many more times than we often think.

To start, during your day focus on identifying situations when you apply *self-determination* – to determine something by yourself, or *self-decision* – to decide by or for yourself. For instance, getting up in the morning is one (no, your alarm clock did not push you out of bed); washing your teeth is another one and drinking a cup of coffee is also one.

At this stage of developing self-leadership it may feel those actions are not the important ones. That's a valid point, but not "the" point. The point is for you to fully assess how you have the capability to be *the boss*; you may not yet apply this capability to the correct situations, or to the important actions, or to increase your choices, etc.

When ready, speed things up a bit. Look at actions slightly more important for you and see when you can decide to be more *the boss* now.

Extra Practice on our Swim 26, the self and the physiology – Let's become really good at cardiac coherence. Cardiac coherence is creating a rhythmic – or coherent – heart rate variability (HRV) which balances our nervous system. This creates a better connection Brain-Brain and Heart-Brain, getting our mind clearer and more focused. For specific research on this check the Heartmath Institute in the USA.

Creating this coherent HRV is straight forward: breathe in and out over cycles of 12 seconds, keeping the inhale and exhale as even as possible, each around 6 seconds of length. The easiest is to count in your head. You can also follow a short video on YouTube (Search for *cardiac coherence*). Repeat this for two to four minutes.

Start first sitting or resting. Then practice while walking or driving. Next do that during meetings, brainstorming sessions, when shopping etc. Make it a habit, especially when you feel low on energy.

A moment of reflection in the aquarium

Seven more swims completed; the habit of regular practice a day-to-day activity, and our fourth step-back moment with our three easy questions:

1) My Favourite Swims in this chapter

2) The Practice Swims I like most and use everyday

3) Write everything which pops up in your head as you read the next question: If I was to describe what the self is, what would that be?

5, Seven Elements to Emotions

It is very important to understand that emotional intelligence is not the opposite of intelligence, it is not the triumph of heart over head – it is the unique intersection of both.

– David Caruso

Fish to fish

As we discovered with our previous chapter, the *self* is like a river. It is a dynamic system, neither transparent nor black, and always in movement. And on that river, emotions float and drift, creating confusion, curiosity, excitement, acceptance, surprise, fear, joy, determination, commitment …

What are emotions actually?

- Why do we have them?
- What do we know about them?
- What is emotional intelligence?
- Can everyone have emotional intelligence?
- How do emotions connect with this dynamic idea of self?
- Are we emotional beings?

Many interesting questions, right?

Pack your bag, food and water and get ready for a trip. It's time to start swimming that river, looking for seven elements; the first seven pieces of knowledge to the world of emotions.

Swim 29: Seven universal emotions

From our Swim 19, we know emotions move us into action; fear may make us fight; sadness may make us hide; etc.

It seems obvious nowadays to see emotion as common to all humans. However, until the 1970s it was considered an absurd idea, and emotions were thought specific to societies and cultures. The capability to feel an emotion was, in fact, mistaken for the cultural convention in expressing that emotion. The change of perspective came with the work of Dr. Paul Ekman[15]. Through the studies of several isolated tribes, from Asia to Americas, Dr. Ekman established the existence of seven basic emotions, which could be recognised by anyone, whatever their culture.

Joy, Sadness, Fear, Disgust, Anger, Contempt, and Surprise.[16]

Each of these emotions is associated with specific facial expressions. A facial marker of Joy would be a genuine or D-smile which involves using 26 muscles. While frowning – a facial marker of anger – consumes more energy with the activation of about 62 muscles. From these seven basic emotions, derivative emotions are developed. Joy can give happiness, and also amusement, relief, peace, wonder, excitement, ecstasy.

Though the seven basic emotions are universal, derivative emotions can be linked to context and culture. For instance, the word Schadenfreude, unique to German, is the expression of pleasure or self-satisfaction that comes from learning of or witnessing the failures or humiliation of another. The emotion of guilt is often associated to Christian culture.

Tip and Practice, Swim 29:

The Tip! There are seven basic emotions, Joy, Sadness, Fear, Disgust, Anger, Contempt, and Surprise. Each of these emotions is associated with facial expressions. Closely observing someone's face can give us factual information on people's emotions.

The Practice! Take a moment to visit the website atlasofemotions.org. Then list every emotion you are familiar with. For several days, pay attention to the emotions you are experiencing. Record their specificities; such as sensations in your body, factual information on the context, thoughts in your mind, etc.; and note what triggers these.

Swim 30: Two steps to a name

Our initial way of experiencing the world around us starts with our five senses (Swim 22); and these senses are activated by triggers or events, either external or internal. An internal trigger can be something I am thinking of. An external trigger can be anything around me, such as a change of temperature, a sound, a picture, someone entering a room, etc.

Emotions, as a manifestation of us experiencing the world, follow the same mechanism; they can be activated by either internal or external triggers. Seeing a car driving towards you at full speed as you cross the street is likely to create fear. However, you won't name it fear straight away. First your body will come up with reactions or responses to the external trigger such as variation of heart rate, blood pressure, muscle tension, brain waves, electrical conductivity of the skin, etc. At the same time, it will produce hormones which will activate neural processes. While all this is happening, you are likely to have jumped onto the kerb. Only then your mind will process that you have just experienced the emotion of fear. We can therefore see that experiencing an emotion happens in two steps.

Learning to identify or recognise an emotion also happens in two steps:

1. Acknowledge an emotion is here by focusing on factual information such as heartbeat, muscle tension, perspiration etc.
2. Then we name or label the emotion – this is sometimes identified as feelings.

The two steps happen very close to each other. Often we do step 2 without having realised step 1 has happened.

Tip and Practice, Swim 30:

The Tip! Emotions manifest first with bodily responses such as, heart rate, blood pressure, blood volume, muscle tension, brain waves, etc. Monitoring bodily responses help us in identifying emotions. Then awareness with the observation of everything within the system me-others-environment help us to identify what triggered the emotions.

The Practice! Building up from Swim 30, when you log the emotions you experience in your notebook, take a moment to separate step 1 and step 2. Do this monitoring actively because you want to condition your brain to keep attention to information linked to emotions.

Swim 31: One emotion several feelings

What if that step 2 from our previous Swim 30, where we name or label the emotion, also known as identifying feelings, was more than one step?

It is 1884 and two scholars, William James and Carl Lange develop an interesting hypothesis, known nowadays as the James-Lange theory:

> *What if the feeling state, the conscious experience of emotion, occurs after the cortex receives signals about changes in our physiological state? What if we could deconstruct the link between emotion, feelings, and mood?*

The emotion becomes the physiological response we experience. It is happening at the body level, and is purely physical, instantly prompting bodily reactions. While the feeling becomes a side product of the emotion, it is how we choose to respond to the emotion based on the interpretation which arises as the brain processes bodily responses. As such, feelings can be impacted by culture, past experiences, expectations, education, etc. As said by Dr. Damasio[17]: *Feelings are mental experiences of body states, which arise as the brain interprets emotions, themselves physical states arising from the body's responses to external stimuli. (The order of such events is: I am threatened, experience fear, and feel horror.).*

Therefore, one emotion could possibly link to several feelings[18].

Tip and Practice, Swim 31:

The Tip! Emotions are the physiological response we experience, while feelings are how we choose to respond to emotions. The full experience of an emotion or feeling is subjective, and can therefore be modified.

The Practice! Let's look at the information you recorded with Swims 29 and 30. For each emotion or feeling listed:

1. Identify what is actually linked to emotions for this focus on factual information linked to bodily response.
2. Identify what is linked to the feelings for this focus on the interpretation of the bodily response.

For example, that butterfly feeling in our belly we have at times? Depending on the context, we may experience it as excitement or stress.

Swim 32: Emotions, mood and physiology

From our Swim 25, we can see a mood as **a set of states of mind**; where a *state of mind* is what's on our mind at a specific moment. Now each state of mind is linked to an emotional state, which is what's going on in our body at a specific moment. We can associate a mood to several emotions and feelings; when we are in a good mood, we may experience joy, excitement, curiosity, peace, etc.

Can a mood impact our physiology? Or our physiology impacts our mood? Could we talk about a system, *mood-states of mind-emotions-physiology*? Then changing one element within the system could influence the full system.

Emotions are physiological responses hardwired into our system which are activated by neural pathways. When our body is damaged and we can't activate the neural pathway, we can't experience the emotion. Hence our physiology has a direct impact on the system mood-states of mind-emotions-physiology. When you're moody and you spend your day moaning on a sofa feeding your body with bad food and limiting oxygen input by lack of movement – here again you have a direct influence on your physiology. Therefore, you have a direct impact on the system mood-states of mind-emotions-physiology. With this Swim, we are strengthening our mind and body connection.

Tip and Practice, Swim 32:

The Tip! Mood-states of mind-emotions-physiology form a system, and changing one element within the system can influence the full system

The Practice! Let's look at how this system mood-states of mind-emotions-physiology reacts to two simple elements: the weather and the people around us. And yes we are building up on Swims 12 and 26.

How is the weather impacting your mood? Do you see a difference between seasons? Between hot and warm weather? How does that impact your physiology?

Next, what about people around you? Can their mood influence yours?

Take a moment to identify other factors impacting your mood.

Swim 33: An emotion, a creation

We have an open system *mood-states of mind-emotions-physiology*; and spontaneously we think emotion, then state of mind, then actions. We follow the system in a passive mode where we start from the experience of the emotions to the actions.

What if we were to follow this system in an active mode?

We would have something like action, then state of mind, then emotion, and the emotion we experience would become a result; something created and chosen.

This is what a good TV drama can do. Here you are, in a good state of mind with friends over, and without warning you start to cry; something you see on screen is able to trigger the physiological reactions of the emotion sadness and you cry. With our Swim 26, we already created an emotion; if you remember we took a pen between our lips for two minutes and with that action we asked our body to release oxytocin, the happiness hormone.

Tip and Practice, Swim 33:

The Tip! The same way that emotions move us out into action; actions can move us in and out of emotions. By choosing a specific state of mind and by paying attention to specific elements, we can influence our physiological reactions, hence our emotions, and then our behaviours.

The Practice! First, pay attention to situations where you spontaneously change your state of mind; for instance, to create the motivation to do something in particular or with someone.

Next, for selected activities decide on a specific state of mind before starting them. For instance, before going to a meeting, choose the state of *being curious* or *being calm*, etc. Note how that changes the quality of your experience, and take a moment to record that in your notebook.

Ready to surprise yourself? Join a laughter yoga session, and see what happens when you ask your body to create the action of laughing … soon enough you will be laughing uncontrollably.

Swim 34: An experience, a structure

We reviewed how experiencing an emotion or feeling is subjective in Swim 31. What if we could add a notion of structure to this subjective experience, with dimensions easy to identify and therefore to modify? Inspired from the work of Cameron-Bandler and Lebeau[19], let's look at a possible structure based on eight separate dimensions defined as follows:

1. **Time Frame**: Sorrow, for example, almost exclusively lies in the past. Helplessness is in the present. Anxiety is in the future.
2. **Model Operators**: These are statements that frame actions and include words such as can/can't, should/shouldn't, could, must, want, like, etc. They imply necessity, possibility, existence, etc.
3. **Comparison**: Based on constant actions to compare past, present, or expected outcomes with expectations or beliefs; usually we either look for similarities or differences.
4. **Chunk Size**: Big chunk thinking looks at the big picture. Small chunk thinking looks for details.
5. **Involvement**: How does one interact with the experience, for instance, self-initiated, self-maintained versus externally created.
6. **Intensity**: The strength of the experience, often rated on a Likert scale from 0 to 10, where 0, nothing, 8, strong, and 10 extreme.
7. **Tempo**: Similar to a musical tempo.
8. **Criteria**: Criteria are the standards we apply in various situations or contexts. In item 3 about comparisons, criteria are the things we use to compare two states or conditions.

Tip and Practice, Swim 34:

The Tip! We can map our subjective experience of feelings using dimensions, such as time frame, involvement, tempo, criteria. And changing the content of any dimension can modify the experience.

The Practice! Take an emotion or feeling you have been experiencing lately and describe it using the eight dimensions above.

For example, the experience of calm, described with our eight dimensions in the order listed above, could give us: *present, existence, matching, small chunk size, mix passive-active, soft intensity, moderate to slow, being in the moment*. If easier, start by focusing only on specific dimensions, for instance time frame, involvement, or criteria.

Swim 35: Four steps to a message

Emotions move us into actions, and actions can move us into emotions. Could we see emotions-actions as a form of dialogue? An emotion would be here to tell us something. And once we have the message, we would then be more capable in finding appropriate behaviours to address the message, the emotion and therefore the situations around all that. We would start to be able to manage emotions and situations.

With our Swim 30, we looked at two steps to name an emotion:

1.   Acknowledge an emotion is here using factual information.
2.   Then name or label the emotion or sometimes the feelings.

Let's add a third and fourth step:

3.   Take a moment to identify what triggered that emotion; was it something external like something you saw or heard, or was it something internal, e.g. a sensation in your body or in your mind. If in your mind, pause and see if you can picture the visual image in your mind which created the internal trigger.
4.   Now ask "What is important about having this emotion now?"

The 5th step, which we will be exploring in a follow-up Swim, will be:

5.   "What can I do to address the message?"

Tip and Practice, Swim 35:

The Tip! Emotions contain messages expressed through our body. When we acknowledge emotions and name them, we start listening to the messages. We are in fact facilitating a dialogue between emotions and actions; an interesting step in our partnership (Swim 21).

The Practice! A quick experiment using steps 3 and 4 above. Keep paying attention to the emotions you experience. Once steps 1 and 2 done, apply step 3, and focus on separating factual information – what you really see, hear, etc. from subjective information – what you think or assume is here. Right now, you are increasing your observations and awareness skills.

Next, bring on step 4, and ask, "What is important about having this emotion?" Repeat that question until you reach a possible action to follow up with.

Some extra swimming for the highly motivated

Feel like swimming further with some added practice? Enjoy!

Extra Practice on Swim 17, maintaining awareness – We can see that observations and awareness are used on a daily basis. Let's practice the skill of observation with our body. It's likely you are sitting at least once a day. Next time you sit, take a moment to notice the chair on which you are sitting. What type of chair is it? Soft? Firm? Cold? Warm? What about the floor which your feet are on? How are your feet on the floor? Can you feel the soles of your shoes? Can you feel your toes moving?

Next, do the same thing while walking. It can be an outdoor walk, for instance from your car to your office, or from the train station to your office. Notice the movements of your legs – maybe the movement of your arms at the same time. You can do that several times a day, for example, as you come back from the water station with a bottle of water to put on your desk.

Lastly, take a moment to note the observations down in your notebook. Focus on factual information.

Extra Practice on Swims 18 and 19, staying relaxed and maintaining movement. Remember your experience with our default posture and go back into it as you read this. You may have noticed how dynamic the posture actually is; every single muscle is used in balance to stay relaxed and standing, and an actual barely visible movement of the muscle allows the sensation to be immobile.

Let's add a fun dimension now: go to a location where many people are passing by – like the entrance to a park or the hall of a train station – and make that default posture in the middle of the location. Observe the flow of people in continuous movement around you. If it feels safe to do so, close your eyes and not only hear the movement, but feel it, and notice how it resonates through your own body, at the same time keep noticing all the tiny movements you experience to remain still, just standing there.

With these extra Swims we are layering knowledge on top of each other. Here we are focusing on the observation skills to build up on our awareness and the monitoring of our system me-others-environment.

A moment of reflection in the aquarium

Seven more Swims completed, exploring how to comprehend emotions and therefore how to influence them or their impact. And now our step-back moment with three easy questions:

1) My Favourite Swims in this chapter

2) The Practice Swims which really make a difference in my perception of emotions

3) The Swims which bring me most out of my aquarium

6, Seven Dives into the River

Exploration is really the essence of the human spirit.

– Frank Borman

Fish to fish

We know the self is like a river, and one aspect of self-leadership is to be okay with this notion of a dynamic self; more than okay actually. One aspect of self-leadership is to become stronger thanks to this notion of a dynamic self. This gives us:

-    Flexibility in actions
-    Adaptability in communication
-    Better understanding of awareness, and how to use it
-    Capability to recover missing information
-    Recognition of the importance of looking ahead, outside of the system me-others-environment
-    Desire to learn and get inspired

Ready to dive into the river and discover more?

Swim 36: Diving for flexibility

As so well written by Frank Borman, "Exploration is really the essence of the human spirit." We are, each one of us, a born explorer (Swim 7), and we start our life through the exploration of the unknown world we are born into, where we enjoy the changes we created (Swim 14).

We also know we are part of the me-others-environment system, and that the most flexible element of a system controls it (see chapter 4).

Exploration, change, and flexibility are three elements feeding each other, where flexibility is about exploring different options by accepting the creation of possible changes. Imagine now having a *change muscle* that can give you extra strength in this capability to explore or flexibility. We will be able to train it; to stretch it as we swim.

If the aquarium is our comfort zone, changing something means jumping out of the aquarium, and trusting we will have the strength to keep swimming on the outside. We need to trust ourselves that everything is going to be okay. Since everything we do is based on activating neural pathways (Swim 26), we want a neural pathway on "trusting ourselves that everything is going to be okay with a change". Developing this neural pathway is what we do when we build this *change muscle*. We practice the habit to trust everything is going to be okay by using simple changes developing a feel for flexibility.

Tip and Practice, Swim 36:

The Tip! The capability to change and to be flexible is like a muscle; the more you practice flexibility, the more you build your change muscle, and the stronger your flexibility becomes.

The Practice! We already started building up our change muscle with our Swim 7, where we told our brain to create the neural pathway "I trust myself when I apply flexibility by creating simple changes".

Let's repeat the same approach. Keep creating small changes in your day-to-day but this time add in your head the sentence "I trust myself when I apply flexibility". Do report in your notebook how easy it is to create these changes. When ready apply the same approach to bigger changes.

Swim 37: Diving for communication

As human beings we are hardwired to be social beings. Leave someone on a desert island, and it is likely this person will create personae to talk to, as beautifully described in the movie, *"Cast Away"*[20].

To be hardwired to be social beings implies communication between social beings is possible. And for communication to happen, we have to assume the existence of a message to be transmitted, where the message is the content of the communication. We need as well ways to deliver this message, for instance, words, a body movement, a wink, a drawing, etc.; these are *channels of communication*. Then, we have a sender, the person creating the message; and of course a receiver, the person receiving the message. We could summarise the communication flow with the picture below, inspired from the mathematician Claude Shannon[21].

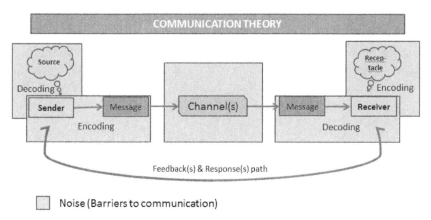

@Talking4good, powerful conversations for powerful actions

Each step is an opportunity for **noises** to be created. Noises are very interesting concepts; they are elements acting as **barriers to communication**. We talk about several types of noises:

1. Technical noise – e.g. the phone line is not very clear.
2. Background or situational noise – e.g. there are roadworks around.
3. Context or environmental noise – e.g. the person is sick with fever.
4. Internal noise – e.g. the person is vision impaired.

All four types of noise will impact the quality of either the transmission or the reception of the message.

The last elements in our model are the source, where the information can be found, and the sender – the person creating the message. Often source and sender are seen as one single element. However, when we study what happens in our brain when we create one sentence, we clearly see many elements at play; such as the health of our brain, the vocabulary we have available, the time we took to collect the proper information in the source, etc. As a sender we actually code the information within the source as a message, and this coding is subject to many ***internal noises***. On the other side of the communication, the receiver has to decode the message before storing it in the receptacle and here, as well, this decoding is subject to many *internal noises*, based on our culture, education, past experiences, expectations, and so on.

The more we understand how we code a message, or decode it, the stronger we are in getting the best out of communication. The same way, the more we recognise the role of noises, as well as their origin, the easier it is to assess their impact and therefore maximise the benefits of communication.

Tip and Practice, Swim 37:

The Tip! The decision of the meaning of the communication is on the receiver's side, and a good communication is not about what is being said, but rather about what is being understood or perceived. When thinking from the receiver's viewpoint we can build stronger messages.

The Practice! With Swims 9 and 23, we focused on identifying factual information in order to avoid assumptions. Going back to factual information is going back to the *source*, and we were in fact exploring our own internal noises.

Let's step up now. Actively look at any communication interaction you had recently. Choose one which went quite poorly, and take a moment to identify all types of noises that were present:

1. Technical noise,
2. Background or situational noise,
3. Context or environmental noise,
4. Internal noise.

Now think about an important communication interaction coming up. What can you do to decrease any of these possible noises? If it's a meeting, it could be the location, the language use, the clothes you choose, etc.

Swim 38: Diving for awareness

A key to self-awareness is an extremely great sense of observations of everything around us (Swim 10); and it starts with the monitoring of the system *me-others-environment*, especially how we interact with it.

When we dive for awareness, we dive for listening to the system. And we are going to explore the word "listening" by looking at its Chinese character. It is drawn below and it consists of five elements, each element a concept by itself:

- Ear – what you use to listen – hear
- King – pay attention as if the other person were King – obey
- Ten and Eye – be observant as if you had ten eyes – heed
- One – Listen with individual attention – attend to
- Heart – listen also with your heart – hearken

What about listening as invited by this Chinese character?

I call this the ***full body listening***, where all our senses become part of the ten eyes, and we therefore listen to body gesture, skin movement, chemistry (even if we are very rarely aware of it), vibration created by the body, e.g. the heart wave, energy projected, tiny facial muscles movement, etc. And of course, still focusing on factual information; however, with undivided attention.

Tip and Practice, Swim 38

The Tip! We strengthen awareness of everything around us with the skill of full body listening. The more aware we are of everything within the system me-others-environment, the easier for us to influence it.

The Practice! Full body listening is another layer built up on our observation skills. In the coming days, take some time to practice it. Sit somewhere and explore listening with undivided attention to every element around, from your guts, your skin, to your environment, as if your body and mind are recording every single pieces of information.

Swim 39: Diving for missing information

We know the recording of our experiences is based on partial and filtered or distorted information, which we translate into words. When we apply self-leadership, in fact, we want to recover this missing information; this allows us to revisit the content of our experiences, and therefore our choices in reacting or comprehending situations.

With this Swim, we are building up on Swims 22, 23 and 27, with a more systematic approach to recovering information. It's an important Swim, not the easiest one, and it starts with exploring the three generic filters of the mind: deletion, distortion and generalisation, by paying attention to the words we use.

1.   The deletion filter

We break down the two million bits of information we receive at every single moment into manageable chunks by hiding in the back of our minds what is not relevant to us in the current moment.

We know we have deleted information when we hear only partial information. When someone says "I'm angry", we have useful information, although information about the root cause of the anger has been deleted. To address the anger and manage the emotions we need to recover "what" the person is angry about. We do that with questions such as "what are you angry about?" Similarly when someone says, "They don't believe me", we are missing the key information and we address it with the question, "Who does not believe you"?

2.   The distortion filter

When we distort we misrepresent the information our senses give us. As we grow and learn, we make judgments about the world around us and accept certain things as being true. Once we form those beliefs, we distort any information that does not support our judgements. We do this automatically in order for new information to conform to, or even reinforce, our own version of reality.

When someone says, "There is no communication between us", and the person is actually talking to you, since talking is a form of communication, you know you have a distortion. To recover the missing information, a good question to ask would be "what do you want to communicate about?"

3.   The generalisation filter

To be able to think fast, our brain generalises information based on one, two, maybe three similar experiences. If every swan we see is white, then we assume all swans are white; until we see a black one. Some generalisations are helpful, such as "all sharks are dangerous", while others can limit our choices and our perspectives, such as "all news on the internet is fake".

When someone says, "nobody ever communicates with me", the word nobody is expressing the generalisation. Here you are, communicating with the person; however, due to the generalisation done, they are unable to see the interaction as communication. You disturb generalisation by showing a counter element; here you could reply, "I am communicating with you, just now, am I not?" or you could look for the missing elements with the following question, "Who would you like to communicate with?"

Filtering is a pattern our brain has been using to allow fast thinking, and survival. Rather than fully analysing each situation, our brain takes shortcuts, leveraging from a knowledge base built over past experiences. But this can lead to incorrect predictions and/or expectations, which is not that far from assumptions. When we apply self-leadership, we focus in recovering missing information and undoing our automatic filtering.

Tip and Practice, Swim 39:

The Tip! The filters in our mind are based on our past experiences so we filter information in a subjective way to match our expectations. One way to recover missing information is to go back to the facts. We usually do that by asking precise questions pointing to the missing information.

The Practice! The focus of this practice is going to be about finding the right question to ask. Listen actively to people's sentences. Note when the sentence you hear is like the tip of the iceberg; if possible note the sentence you hear. Next, look back at the sentence and think about the questions you would like to ask to get the background information that is hidden. For this we may want to think about what is assumed or unprecise.

Next is much more interesting. Listen to your own sentences and start noticing when they are incomplete, giving only partial information. Think then about the question to ask to challenge your own sentences.

Swim 40: Diving for the horizons

Here you are about to build a small bridge over a river. What approach would you rather choose?

Approach 1 – Stand with your back to the river, throwing stones, wood, or any other material over your head and behind you into the river.

Approach 2 – Identify a point on the other side which seems to be a good direction to aim for, and then align the elements needed to build the bridge with that point.

It is likely you said Approach 2. Interestingly enough, in real life, Approach 1 is the most chosen one. It seems we often hope to go somewhere only looking at our past; the river behind us.

Applying self-leadership means applying Approach 2, and means finding the horizon to aim for. It may be something really precise, like a goal or an objective, or it can be an impression; something giving you an overall sense of direction. Whatever is right for you, this point on the horizon is here to give the energy and direction to actions or movement you create in life.

Tip and Practice, Swim 40:

The Tip! Looking at the horizon is about identifying something ahead of us which can give energy and direction to movements we create in life. This helps harness all our resources toward the same direction.

The Practice! We start with physically rediscovering the notion of horizon:

1. Stretch your eyes switching from *close focus*, such as looking at your phone, to *far focus*, like looking through a window.
2. Ensure rooms you work in have windows, and these windows give you the capability to look a good distance away.
3. Create opportunities to go to places where you can have a view, your eyes stretching over the panorama, looking as far as possible. As you look further and further, breathe with all your body, taking more and more space.
4. As soon as you can, implement the habit of day-dreaming, letting your eyes look towards the horizons; and enjoy it!

Swim 41: Diving for learning

Learning is happening in our brain. It is, in fact, happening through the creation of neural processes which we can explore through five stages[22]:

1. **Unconscious incompetence**: you do not know the skills exist hence you do not know you have no competence in it. For instance, you've never seen a bicycle, you do not know bicycles exist, and you do not know cycling is a skill you do not have.

2. **Conscious incompetence**: now you know about the skill, and you know you do not have it. You saw your friend cycling. At the same time you discovered bicycles exist, you discovered cycling is a skill and that you do not have the skills. You know you are incompetent, however you can now move to learning the skill.

3. **Conscious competence**: you have the skill but you have to consciously think of every step you do to perform the skill. Staying with our bicycle example, you can cycle now, but you still have to think balance, pushing on the pedal, focusing on the road, etc.

4. **Unconscious competence**: you have a skill and you can apply it without thinking about it. When you now pick up your bicycle, you jump on it, pedal away, talking with friends at the same time, etc.

5. **The expertise**: you have a skill, you can apply it without thinking, and at the same time you can switch off your automatic reaction to expertly choose a precise way of applying the skill. Richard Restak will simply say, *"In order to achieve superior performance in a chosen field, the expert must counteract the natural impulse to gain an automated performance as soon as possible."*[23]

Tip and Practice, Swim 41:

The Tip! Learning is a process. Recognising skills in others is part of the process, which moves us from stage 1 to stage 2 above. When we have gone through stage 2 and recognise a skill in someone, we have started the process of acquiring the skill in question.

The Practice! Take a moment to list either skills or competencies you have and assess at what stages in the learning process you are. Next for each skill, give a priority number from 1 to 4. For every skill listed as priority 1, what would help you to go to the next level if you knew what would that be? As you read these two questions, list everything coming to mind – everything, even if it does not make sense.

Swim 42: Diving for inspiration

Maybe we are just learning machines? Maybe, our survival instinct is just a compulsory need for learning? Some theories debate whether humans ever reach adulthood since we keep our faculty to play like children. This propensity to play may actually be the evolution which has allowed humans always to learn. Who knows? However this drive for learning is in itself an amazing skill of self-leadership. It implies a constant strive for improvement.

An easy way of learning is imitation; we could even argue all learning goes through imitation. Therefore one good way to acquire skills is to imitate role models, using them as a source of inspiration.

When looking for role model, think about three questions:

1. What makes you choose them as a role model?
2. What is important to you about having them as a role model?
3. What do you want to learn from them?

When I look for role model to inspire me in my development of self-leadership, I may either think of a skill first, and look for someone that is demonstrating this skill; or I may be inspired by someone, and then take a moment to assess what specifically draw my attention or inspired me. And then I imitate, to the point that I may even mimic body movement, in order to create changes in impressions and actions, using the body-mind connection effect.

Tip and Practice, Swim 42:

The Tip! Having role models to imitate give us directions to follow, and can help developing our skills into competencies.

The Practice! Look for people, or personages, who truly inspire you. They can be alive, deceased or even fictional characters. Once you have identified some role models, take a moment to review:

1. What makes you choose them as a role model.
2. What is important to you about having them as a role model.
3. What do you want to learn from them?
4. Then, observe them, and step by step start modelling their attitudes or actions – by modelling we mean to start doing things as they do.

Some extra swimming for the highly motivated

Feel like swimming further with some added practice? Enjoy!

Extra Practice on our Swim 36, diving for flexibility by building up our change muscles a bit more – Developing flexibility starts with very simple things, as simple as taking the time every day to do something in a slightly different way. You can decide to lock your door or write with your non-dominant hand; you can take a different route to go to work; you can buy a different washing-up liquid; you can change how you greet people from a "Hello" to something else; and so on.

Do make these changes small and do make them often. Like the muscle of an athlete, you want your brain to practice regularly in order to build up stamina. When ready move a level up and start implementing slightly bigger changes. Note how you remain the same person, though doing things in a slightly or very different way.

Take a moment then to reflect on what is easier, between:

1. Experimenting with changes we create, or
2. Accepting people around us being surprised and sometimes judgemental of changes we create.

Extra Practice on Swim 42, diving for inspiration by modelling role models – Rather than just being inspired by people we meet or have heard of, we can decide to look actively for role models.

How do you do that?

1. Think about a skill or competency you would really want to develop and strengthen.
2. Specifically hunt for someone who manifests this skill or competency (and yes it can be someone you will never meet).
3. Start modelling this person.

The same way that competition swimmers all have slightly different ways of swimming, different people will apply skills with different style. Look for several role models with the same skill, in order to observe several ways of achieving competency in that skill. Then choose the style which works best for you.

What about now being a role model for someone else?

A moment of reflection in the aquarium

Seven Swims completed, but not just swims, actual dives where we focus on deepening knowledge and implementing stronger habits. Let's now step back with three easy questions:

1) My Favourite Swims in this chapter

2) What about the Swim on communication? What is the most important information I learned with this Swim?

3) What about the Swim on horizons? Write whatever comes up in your head as you read the following question (you can draw if easier). What would you like to see on your horizon at the moment?

7, Seven Habits to Partner Up

The self is a perpetually recreated neurobiological state.

– Antonio Damasio

Fish to fish

Self-leadership is having a developed sense of who we are, what we can do, where we are going – coupled with the ability to influence our communication, emotions and behaviours on the way to getting there.

With chapters one, two and three, we established a foundation where we reached self-leadership Level 1. With chapters four, five, six, we built up our knowledge exploring the notion of the self, communication, emotions, and behaviours. We also established how we are an element within several interconnected systems, such as the *me-others-environment* system, or the *mood-states of mind-emotions-physiology* one. We could add the following: the *body-mind* system, the *emotions-behaviours-actions* system, the *body-environment* system, etc. And within all these systems, what is going to make THE difference is our ability to influence them using communication, emotions and behaviours.

Charles Swindoll, an American clergyman, wrote this simple and still extraordinary sentence: *"Life is 10% what happens to you and 90% how you react to it."* Identifying what is the 10%, which is the factual information, from the remaining 90%, which is our interpretation or reactions, gives us a lot more choices and options on how to deal with the 10% and therefore how to influence where these 10% bring us.

One attitude is really going to help us here, the attitude to partner up with ourselves (Swim 21). Let's explore seven habits to a strong partnership with oneself. These seven habits are going to really impact the 90% we just talked about.

Swim 43: Choose your words

If you are like most people, you are speaking to yourself on a regular basis. True. It is not a perfect dialogue "Dear me, how are you today", "I'm fine, and you, ready to go for a walk?" and so on … It is rather thoughts passing by, like a continuous monologue; and to build this monologue we use words.

It is the year 1996 – yes more than 20 years ago – and John A. Bargh, Mark Chen, and Lara Burros decide to trick students from Yale University. Inviting them to test their English proficiency and literary capacity, they give them jumbled sentences to re-construct as quickly as possible. Most students excelled proudly. But this is not the real test. The real test is a measurement on how fast students are walking back from the test room to the elevator after having completing the literary exercise. The control group is given "neutral" words, while the others are given specific sentences including words such as *old*, *grey*, *lonely*, *bingo*, *wrinkle*. Guess what? All but the control group had a slower pace. They simply began to walk just as elderly people would. The simple action of reading words associated with elderly people made them act old.

This is called "Automaticity of Social Behaviour" and is linked to the concept of ***priming***. Words are not only labels of our experience, they are pre-loaded with meaning, and the words we choose have an impact on our overall mood and state of mind. In fact, each bit of information our mind receives – via colour, pictures, artwork, etc. – can have a priming effect.

Tip and Practice, Swim 43:

The Tip! Words are pre-loaded with meaning and the words we hear or use influence our experiences and behaviours. Changing our choice of words when talking to oneself can change our perceptions of who we are, and therefore our motivation, mood and enthusiasm, etc.

The Practice! Let's follow up on our Swim 21 where you took a moment to listen to the words you use when talking about you or to yourself. Go back to your list now. Are you happy with those words? What about replacing now some of them with stronger words, pre-loaded with the intention you want to achieve. What about, starting today, deciding to use words which really echo what you want to say. Go ahead, write these new chosen words in your notebook, now.

Swim 44: Work with the team

It is interesting to note that, depending on context, we do things differently. When managing a project at work, you may have a very precise methodology with a clear calendar timeline defined. In this specific context, it is to your advantage to become time oriented and structured. However, as the weekend arrives and your friends contact you to organise something, you reply, "let's just meet and see what happens". In that specific context, you choose to apply a different style, and to become moment oriented. You now plan your next vacation; you have a limited number of days and you want to see the three "must-see" sights of the area. You book accommodation and transportation to be 100% confident this will happen, but you leave everything else to the feeling of the moment. In this last context, you choose to again apply a different style, an actual mix between the first two. It is possible that you prefer one style to the others; still all styles are good, and all styles are something you can do.

All these different styles or ways of being for specific contexts are, in fact, aspects of who we can be; they are like mini personae, each one addressing specific needs for specific contexts.

Is the fact of being able to do things differently, in order to address specific situations and contexts, changing who we are? Of course not! We remain the same person; we just show the ability to adapt and navigate within different contexts. The more comfortable we are navigating from one context to another, the more flexibility we develop and can apply.

Tip and Practice, Swim 44:

The Tip! All these kind of personae, which are simply our capability in doing things applying different methodologies, are members of our self-team. And, it is well known; a team is greater than the sum of its parts.

The Practice! Time management, as seen above, is a skill often approached differently at work, at home, on vacation. Take a moment to review how you manage time. Note what style is more natural for you and therefore less *energyvore*.

Look now for other activities where, depending on the context, you may adopt different styles. Here again note the more natural style for you. Next step, of course, is to practise the other styles to build flexibility.

Swim 45: Eat, rest, sleep

So far, we partner up within our mind, all the different aspects of our character working together as a team. Time now to partner up with our physical being, with three easy steps – eat well and balance, rest your muscles and your brain, and sleep.

1. **Eat well and balance:** You remember how we are only a collection of neural processes (Swim 26). Actually there is a lot more than that; there are quite a lot of bones, muscles, and organs; and all these are made of elements such as oxygen, hydrogen, carbon, calcium and so on. To keep all these up and running we need food; good quality food.

2. **Rest your muscles and your brain:** We need rest to process the food, create energy, and renew body elements. Resting the brain is done with daydreaming or activities where you do not actively use your brain.

3. **Sleep:** And lastly sleep is in fact key to a well-balanced brain. Without sleep, step by step your brain stops being able to process experiences: to learn, to create new memories, or to consolidate them. When preparing for an examination with a high content of memory work, rather than working continuously, you are better off studying for short periods of time. And between each period have about 15 minutes of either physical activity or sleep. This will help consolidate memory and therefore learning.

Tip and Practice, Swim 45:

The Tip! Our body condition and health have a direct influence on our physiology and with it our possible choice of behaviours and actions. Take care of your body in order to take care of your mind and your cool with three steps: eat, rest, and sleep.

The Practice! With our Swim 26, we already explored step 1 above. Let's dig on to step 3 today. On average an adult needs between 6 to 8 hours sleep. How regular is your sleeping schedule? How easily are you falling asleep? How rested are you feeling when waking up? If you answer "Not really" to the three questions, maybe talk with a physician as you may be experiencing poor resting periods.

To improve how we rest, the first step is to implement a regular sleeping schedule. Note your chosen schedule, and respect it.

Swim 46: Be at cause

Somehow we are always the boss of us (Swim 3); and yes, that is not an easy statement to take on board. We are in fact extremely good at making excuses. If you do not believe me, go and enjoy listening to Larry Smith's TED talk *"Why you will fail to have a great career"*[24].

Maybe finding excuses is a way to protect who we are? **Finding excuses** is a behaviour in itself, and since every behaviour has a positive intention (Swim 28), *finding excuses* also has a positive intention. Once we find that positive intention, two things are possible:

1. We can identify other options to achieve the same intention.
2. We can learn from the experience.

Being at cause is about seeing these other options, and therefore unlocking the possibility to learn from the experience.

Not all clear yet? Let's have a test then.

Are you *at cause* right now as you read this book?

To decide, try these very simple questions:

Have you – yourself – decided to read this book?   *"Yes/No"*

Do you claim the ownership in picking up this   *"Yes/No"*
book and reading it?

It's likely you answered "Yes" to both questions. In the context of reading this book, you are actually at cause, claiming the ownership of the action you took to read the book.

We defined *being at cause* in relation to *being in effect* – and yes I borrowed this terminology from NLP[25]. If you remain *in effect*, you are seeing yourself as a *receiver of the situation*, and therefore as someone with limited capability in changing the situation. This is associated with the perception of having no control and people in effect tend to use wordings such as "being a victim", "life is unfair", "it's happening to me".

When you move to *being at cause*, you take a stand and decide to accept some ownership in the situation you're facing. By taking that stand, you actually give yourself options to do something about the situation, and to create actions. You move from being a receiver to becoming an *actor* or even an *active agent*.

If the idea of being at cause is not so easy to accept, you may be misunderstanding it for *being the cause*. The two expressions are very different. *Being at cause* is about taking ownership of what could happen next in our life. It's about looking for available options and creating movement by creating actions. And yes, it uses our innate capability of applying autonomy (Swim 2).

Let's bring this to developing self-leadership.

Since we want to be able to *influence our communication, emotions and behaviours on the way to getting there*, we want to put ourselves in positions where we have power to act and influence. This happens when we move at cause.

Tip and Practice, Swim 46:

The Tip! Being at cause is becoming an active agent. We do that by taking ownership for what happens in our life. Often the simple fact of choosing to act moves us to being at cause.

The Practice! With this swim we moved from the wording "being a victim", where victims are powerless, to the wording "becoming an active agent", where agents are powerful.

An easy first step is to implement a simple change of vocabulary in our internal dialogue. When in a challenging situation, repeat in your head "I am an active agent" like a mantra. This will help your mind in seeing options. Here we are building up on Swims 27 and 43.

Being at cause explored several capabilities of self-leadership. Let's focus on the following four: decision-making, autonomy, being an active agent, taking ownership. Note these four down in your notebook. And now, during your days ahead, pay attention to when you are applying one of them; and when you are not. When you are not, ask yourself, "How would it be if I was applying (…)? What would happen next?"

Swim 47: Practice focus

How we experience the world is a fascinating story, weaving a combination of events, neural processes, chemicals and experiences; and still using barely 0.1% of the information we have in our brain.

How could we use more? How could we create a stronger partnership with ourselves? How could we leverage from this notion of congruency we discovered in Swim 27? How could we use the shortcuts of our brain, like priming, to our advantage (Swim 43)?

The answer is easy: we practice *focus*. We identify a direction to aim towards as we did in Swim 40 – identifying horizons, and we describe it choosing our words carefully in order to *say it the way we want it*.

By *saying it the way you want it*, you create four actions:-

1. You give a direct direction to your unconscious mind (or non-cognitive brain), addressing shortcuts identified in Swim 22, i.e., the filtering.
2. You tap into congruency by thinking the walk (Swim 27).
3. You prime yourself for achieving what you want (Swim 43).
4. You harness both the cognitive and non-cognitive capabilities of your brain by giving them exactly the same information to focus on.

Tip and Practice, Swim 47:

The Tip! Always say things the way you want it.

The Practice! Let's say you want to avoid getting angry with someone. Rather than thinking "I don't want to get angry", focus on what you want to see happening instead and say, for instance, "I want to remain calm" or "I want to be compassionate" or "I want to remain cool", etc.

When you say things the way you want it, do make sure:

1. To use the present tense,
2. To use an affirmative sentence,
3. And lastly, to include "I" in your sentence.

Throughout your day, listen to your thoughts and words. Note when you *say things the way you want it*, and note when you do not. When you don't; pause, and take a moment to rephrase your sentence until you *say what you want to achieve, the way you want it*.

Swim 48: Use metaphors

Our brain is a fascinating piece of biology. It is split into several cortexes, and many lobes – frontal, parietal, occipital and temporal. Each cortex is mapped into functional areas (aka Brodmann's areas). It has two cerebral hemispheres, connected by commissural nerve tracts, the largest one being the corpus callosum. It can process words and languages and it can process images and art. And even though the split right-left hemisphere is far from being as black and white as we initially thought, we clearly have two very different ways of processing experiences; one way being very verbal, sequential and analytical; the other more global, holistic and visual-spatial.

Somehow our brain speaks two languages. However, in our day to day lives, most of us focus actively on using only one language – the rational one. And this means using only part of our brain capability.

To develop fluency in the second language of our brain, which is the symbolic language, we practice storytelling and the art of metaphors. If you are familiar with the world of Carl Jung, this is what we do with active imagination. If you are familiar with the world of Milton Erickson, this is also what we do with hypnotherapy and indirect suggestions.

Tip and Practice, Swim 48:

The Tip! Our brain speaks two languages, a rational one with words and a symbolic one with images. To fully use our brain we want to develop fluency in both languages. Metaphors using images will connect with our brain at a symbolic level engaging non-cognitive processes.

The Practice! For some of us, developing the symbolic fluency may feel strange. Be patient and play with it.

First we draw (and yes poor quality drawing is fine).

Take a pen and paper and ask this neutral question: "What I like to see happening around me look like what?" As you read it, draw whatever comes to mind. To help you, you can first write words, moving to drawing those words as step 2. What is important is to express whatever comes to your mind unfiltered. It may not make any sense, and that's okay. These are symbols which your non-cognitive brain uses, and you are now learning this new language.

Swim 49: Love actually

If you were to search on the internet for "rice love hate experience" you may be surprised by the numbers of hits and by the experience itself: a jar of rice turning mouldy under the influence of the sentence – "I hate you".

Love is a strong emotion, and loving oneself is a strength you want to enjoy. Even though you may not see it yet, you have always been there for yourself, every single day of your life (Swim 21). And to strengthen our love for ourselves, we are going to use five easy steps:

1. We learn to be patient and accept to take our time.
2. We delay gratification, and we think negotiation and win-win situations for all aspects of ourselves.
3. We eat, rest, and sleep (yes, this is Swim 45).
4. We recognise the effort, and appreciate making this effort.
5. We respect ourselves.

Step 4 is actually a life changing one, and is an important step towards developing what we call a *growth mindset*. It is the difference between *doing the best* and ***doing our personal best***. We learn more when putting an effort into doing something, rather than just doing something easily. And developing this capability to make an effort, and recognise it, builds up stamina, resilience and determination.

Tip and Practice, Swim 49:

The Tip! Strong self-leadership implies a strong respect and love of oneself. A strong beginning is to acknowledge your efforts and being okay with failures, as long as you learn from them and you keep trying.

The Practice! We are going to borrow this exercise from Louise Hayes' work. Every day, regularly repeat this sentence, "I love, respect and forgive myself", using three different ways:

1. "I love, respect and forgive myself"
2. "YOUR FIRSTNAME love, respect and forgive her/himself"
3. "YOUR FIRSTNAME LASTNAME love, respect, and forgive her/himself"

Note into your notebook, either as words or images, any of your impressions as you repeat these sentences.

Some extra swimming for the highly motivated

Feel like swimming further with some added practice? Enjoy!

Extra Practice on Swim 43, choose your words – Listen to your internal dialogue, note the sentences you use, and take a moment to rewrite the ones not supporting the idea of "partnering up".

For instance: "You can be so stupid" can become "You're not as smart as you need to be yet" or "You will be smarter next time" etc. "You always get it wrong" becomes "You will get it right next time" etc.

You are merging *choosing your words* with *saying things the way you want them to happen*, giving you focus and skills to work on.

Extra Practice on Swim 47, practice focus – To say things the way you want it, we create sentence using three key points:

1. We use the present tense.
2. We use an affirmative sentence.
3. We include "I" in the sentence.

"I do not want to be afraid" can become then "I want to be brave"; "I want to speak up"; "I want to be heard and listened to"; etc.

"I do not want to hesitate" can become "I want to speak clearly and loudly"; "I want to be precise"; "I want to be precise and assertive"; etc.

Extra Practice on Swim 48, use metaphors – Let's say you have a problem and you want to find a solution. Take a pen and a paper and make yourself comfortable to be able draw or write. As you read the following questions, either draw or write whatever comes into your mind, unfiltered:

1. "To find a solution to my problem" is like what?
2. Is there anything else about that "finding a solution to my problem"?

These two "Clean Language" questions lack precision on purpose, using neutral words like that or what, in order to avoid pre-framing our mind for an answer. The more neutral your language, the freer you are from presuppositions and assumptions.[26]

A moment of reflection in the aquarium

Some disruptive Swims, right. Sit and relax now, and step back for a moment with three easy questions:

1) My Favourite Swims in this chapter

2) What do I like most about our Swim, practice Focus?

3) What about the Swim, love actually? Read the following question, "Respecting myself is like what?", and write whatever comes to mind.

8, Seven Skills to Emotional Intelligence

Unless you are prepared to give up something valuable you will never be able to truly change at all, because you'll be forever in the control of things you can't give up.

– Andy Law

Fish to fish

Here we are, rich of seven new habits to strengthen our self-leadership. And we need that. Rivers are not always calm and easy to follow; they can get muddy, cold, rough, tricky, clear, warm, fast, limpid, quiet, noisy, etc. How we swim through life is diverse. Using the work of Howard Gardener, an American development psychologist, we can explore our experiences through nine types of intelligence[27]:

1. **Bodily-kinesthetic** or body-smart – the coordination of mind and body.
2. **Spatial** or picture-smart – the ease to visualise the world in 2D and 3D.
3. **Naturalist** or nature smart – the comprehension of nature and the system man-nature.
4. **Musical** or sound-smart – the ease to work with sounds and recognise them.
5. **Linguistic** or word-smart – the facility to find the right words to express our ideas.
6. **Logical-mathematical** or rational-smart – the ease in using rational thinking.
7. **Intra-personal** or self-smart – the acceptance and appreciation of who we are.
8. **Inter-personal** or people-smart – the acceptance and appreciation of others.
9. **Existential** or life-smart – the comprehension of the meaning of life.

We develop each of these intelligences when strengthening self-leadership. For instance, our Swims 43 and 47 work on linguistic intelligence.

Let's focus for this chapter on Intra-personal and Inter-personal intelligences, which are specific to emotional intelligence. Intra-personal intelligence is about how we handle ourselves, our personal skills and competencies and yes we are going to link this to self-awareness. Inter-personal intelligence looks at how we manage our relationships with others; our social skills and competencies.

Combine both and we get emotional intelligence, or the art of both cultivating emotional balance and knowing how to use this emotional balance.

Let's unpack seven skills to emotional intelligence.

Swim 50: Self-awareness

Self-awareness literally means the awareness of the self, and it implies a comprehension of what (or who) is the self, and a capability to be aware. With our Swim 10, we defined self-awareness as being done by monitoring the system me-others-environment. To perform this monitoring we have observations, then this concept of full body listening. Let's now add the complementary concept of uptime and downtime, where:

- Uptime means to focus our attention on to everything external to us
- Downtime to focus our attention on to everything internal to us

Remember our Swim 35 – four steps to a message? Downtime is used when performing steps 1 and 2, which are the monitoring of the *me*; while both Uptime and Downtime are used for step 3 and 4. Similarly when looking at our Swim 31 – one emotion, several feelings – both Uptime and Downtime are used; while our Swim 32 relies more on Downtime.

The monitoring of the system me-others-environment is a permanent back and forth between Uptime and Downtime. With this monitoring we gather factual information and indications on our emotional triggers, where an emotional trigger is an event, either external or internal, which leads us to experience the emotion.

Tip and Practice, Swim 50:

The Tip! We continuously alternate uptime-downtime to effectively monitor the system me-others-environment. With this monitoring we gather factual information on our emotional triggers.

The Practice! To drive or cycle safely we have to be Uptime. While we focus on completing a task, putting all our attention onto it, we move to Downtime. First, we practice recognising Uptime and Downtime.

During your day, take a moment to note when you are spontaneously Uptime, and when you are spontaneously Downtime. To spot the difference, ask yourself where your attention is: to yourself and your actions or to the outside. See how easily you navigate between both. Next, choose specifically to use one or the other. What does it change to the experience?

Actively make it a habit to alternate the two.

Swim 51: Self-regulation

When we talk about self-regulation, we are talking about the regulation of the self. And the self being a dynamic concept (Swim 7), the regulation of the self is likely to be dynamic, using flexibility and adaptability to situations and contexts. This self-regulation is going to help cultivating emotional balance.

Let's go back to our Swim 35 – four steps to a message – and its step 4. Understanding what is important about an emotion, and about experiencing it, gives us something to learn and this learning creates choices. As the Buddhist's way says *"It's not that you should have no emotion, but rather you should check out other options that would deal with the situation appropriately and effectively."* Self-regulation can be seen as the four consecutive steps we explored with Swim 35 plus a 5th one:

1. Acknowledge an emotion is here – observing factual information.
2. Name or label the emotion – or sometimes the feelings.
3. Take a moment to identify what triggered it – an external or internal trigger?
4. Ask, "What is important about having this emotion now?" or "What positive information am I to learn from this emotion/experience?"
5. And now, "What can I do to address the message?", "What other reactions can I choose to achieve the same result?"

Tip and Practice, Swim 51:

The Tip! Self-regulation starts with self-awareness, and ends with flexibility and adaptability. We focus on developing curiosity to find multiple emotional options to choose from to react to situations and context.

The Practice! Let's build up from Swim 35, exploring further this question "What is important about having this emotion now?" Take specific situations where you want to explore the emotions experienced. As you look back at one situation, ask "What was important about having this emotion at that time?" Repeat the question several times until you have identified all possible answers. Next, rephrase those answers saying it the way you want it, with Swim 47. If answers come up as metaphors, fine, go back to Swim 48 to work with it.

Swim 52: Mental states

Self-regulation can be *energyvore,* and can ask a lot of our brain, especially our pre-frontal cortex where focus, determination and willpower happens. This is one of the reasons why sleeping is so important. Sleeping, flooding the brain with cerebrospinal fluid, acts like a cleaning solution helping the brain in resourcing its energy[28]. Be safe though. The more you practice self-regulation, the easier it becomes.

Until now, we practiced self-regulation in a reactive way; in reaction to situations. What about using self-regulation in a proactive way? What about choosing the emotions we want to experience ahead of time?

Building up now on our Swim 33, we are going to widen our proactive capabilities, by leveraging from the notion of state of mind, which I will call **mental states**. And we are going to build up a library of possible mental states to go to, each state calling on specific skills, actions, emotions, and physiology.

In fact, we have already started with that when implementing the seven habits of our survival kit. They defined our **self-leadership default mental state**. If exploring Buddhist philosophy (Tibetan's model), you may be surprised to find an official list of 51 different mental states to work with.

Tip and Practice, Swim 52:

The Tip! A mental state is linked to specific skills, actions, emotions, and physiology. By choosing to go into a mental state, we specifically call onto its properties. We build our library of mental states with naturally experienced mental states and constructed ones

The Practice! Review the list of the mental states established with Swim 33. These are spontaneous ones and the first elements of your library. Now, review Swim 42 practice, and the role models listed. It is likely that "What is important to you about having those role models" can be associated to specific mental states. Give a name to each of these new mental states. These are the second elements of your library.

Next, to each of these mental states, associate a strong image. When calling this image up in your mind, enjoy experiencing the chosen mental state.

Swim 53: Motivation

Like the word emotion, motivation comes from the Latin *movere,* and motivation is about the creation of movement. What we often forget is that motivation is a brief operation, a brief reaction that starts the movement. The truly interesting question is how to maintain that motivation. And usually this is following a four step process:

1. We respond to a trigger – either something we see, hear, taste, smell or feel; external or internal to us.
2. We associate this trigger to mental pictures where we spontaneously see what would be the result of taking action.
3. When that mental picture matches some criteria – sometimes hidden in our mind – we initiate motivation and start acting.
4. With the action created, we generate emotion or feelings, and to maintain our motivation, we need this emotion to still support our step 3, which is like an ongoing "check" at the back of our mind.

We can recognise how the self-awareness we develop plays an important role in step 1 and 3. Step 2 happens often without much thinking, and the mental picture we see will either move us away from or toward something. To facilitate *maintaining motivation* you want the image in step 2 to move you toward something; then the more you act, the closer you get to results and the stronger your motivation becomes.

Tip and Practice, Swim 53:

The Tip! Each of us has motivation strategies and whatever they are they include a feedback loop (step 3 above). To maintain motivation you want to create positive feedback loops moving you toward something.

The Practice! To be motivated towards or away from something comes spontaneously, and is often linked to context. Look at several things you did recently; and note the direction you swam to. What is *away from* or *toward* something? Focus on situations where you noted swimming away from. From each of them, ask several times, "When swimming away from, what am I going towards?" Write down your thoughts.

What about now adding an extra step, and writing it the way you want it using Swim 47? You have now converted a motivation away from to a motivation toward something. Neat, right?

Swim 54: Empathy

With the word empathy we are entering in to the area of interpersonal intelligence, and moving our focus toward the others within our extended system me-others-environment. What happened to others is likely to influence the 10% we talked about in chapter seven, i.e., what happens to us; while our relationship with others is going to influence the other 90%; our reactions to situations.

Empathy is the awareness of the needs and feelings of others. Experiencing empathy helps us comprehend how others may experience life, as well as creating a stronger connection with them. The myth of understanding we unpacked with our Swim 9 is a tool of empathy. When we move to comprehend someone's situation, we are acknowledging the person's emotions and feelings; and we respect and accept them even though we may not agree with the person or the overall situation. The awareness we have been developing through self-awareness, while using full body listening or when practising uptime, is another tool of empathy. With it we are giving undivided attention to others in order to notice factual information based sometimes on very subtle cues; like non-verbal ones, facial micro-expressions, or missing verbal information.

Our ability to experience empathy is partially linked to us having mirror neurons. Those neurons fire up when we watch others doing something, and this kind of creates an "As If" virtual 3D experience in our mind. This allows us to experience what we would feel if we were in their shoes.

Tip and Practice, Swim 54:

The Tip! Experiencing empathy helps us comprehend how others may experience life. Empathy makes us stronger at communicating and connecting with others.

The Practice! Let's go back to doing Uptime (Swim 50). This time, keep your focus solely on people. Pay particular attention to gesture, tone of voices, words, and facial expressions. Get into the habit to always pay attention to these sources of factual information.

In addition, every day stretch your facial muscles for 2 to 5 minutes. The more flexibility in your own facial muscles, the stronger you will be at identifying other facial expressions.

Swim 55: Social skills

You, me, your neighbours, we are all hardwired to be social beings. This means the need and use of communication is instilled in us. Deprive anyone of communication and they go crazy. Deprive a child of communication and its psychological and mental development slows down, or even stops. Influencing, conflict negotiations, team leadership, change management, collaboration, cooperation, charisma; these are important social skills and they all involve communication in one form or another.

However, good communication is not so much about what is being said but rather about what is being understood or perceived. Right, this is a two-way effort, with 50-50 done on both the sender's and the receiver's side. Still the receiver has the upper hand and it's easy to see how applying empathy can make us much stronger in building good communication skills. Let's now look closely at channels of communication; which are all the available ways to communicate our message. There are many:

- Verbal – the what, words, languages,
- Non-verbal – the how, body, voice, gesture,
- Situational – the where,
- Temporal – the when, and so on.

Even your choice of clothes can be a channel of communication. The rule of thumb is simple: either set the communication channel as neutral as possible, or cleverly charged with intentions. But, always assess its impact.

Tip and Practice, Swim 55:

The Tip! To create good communication, aim at reducing as much interference as possible and leverage from any available channels of communication; be it a room, a time, an ambiance, a gesture, a facial expression, a choice of clothes, a choice of format, etc.

The Practice! How many channels of communication are you actively using? Think back and look at recent situations involving important communications. Focus on the channels of communication you have been using without actively thinking about them. And yes your attitude will be one of them; your mental state on a specific day will be another; your current emotions a third one, etc. Note your observations in your notebook. What ideas does that give you?

Swim 56: Courage

You remember our Swim 35 – four steps to a message? Fear, like any other emotion, is a message. It usually gives us information on possible dangers to watch out for. Fear acts as a reminder to be sharp, smart and strong, and therefore a motivator to develop courage.

We have many different types of courage. It could be: the courage to acquire new skills, the courage to be assertive, the courage to recognise we are not there yet, the courage to be different, the courage to act, the courage to improve and become the next bigger version of ourselves, and so on.

What about seven steps to develop courage?

1. When you experience fear, ask, "What is the positive intention behind this fear?" (Swims 28, 35). It will share a light on skills to work on.
2. Practice focus and say things the way you want it (Swim 47), to work on the skills to develop and the projected outcomes (Swim 40).
3. Use your survival kit (Chapter 3): observe, stay in the moment, and be factual. Being in the moment avoids anxiety (Swim 34).
4. Add self-regulation to keep fear at a certain level (Swim 51).
5. Partner-up to find options to address fear and its messages (Swim 44).
6. Keep your growth mindset hat on. Focus on the effort and learn as you go (Swims 41, 46).
7. Build up a mental state and the image going with it for the *courageous you*. Use words, metaphors, drawings (Swims 48, 52).

Showing courage is a skill as much as a builder of skills. Fear tells us we may be getting out of the box; courage helps us to actually do it; and our unpacked myth of confidence (Swim 13) gives us the strength to do it.

Tip and Practice, Swim 56:

The Tip! We have been practising courage since birth. And to move from fear to courage, we focus on skills to develop and outcomes to reach.

The Practice! Think of situations where you may have experienced fear or anxiety, and pass them through the seven steps process above. Focus first on steps 1 and 2; then use steps 3 to 6 to give you strength as you manage the situation. With step 7, we think long-term and we build-up mental states images for our global library that we can call the skills of courage any time we need (Swim 52).

Some extra swimming for the highly motivated

Feel like swimming further with some added practice? Enjoy!

Extra Practice on Swim 54, empathy – With this "perceptual positions" exercise, we practice a several-steps approach to see situations from three different perspectives. For this, we use four different spatial positions in a room to facilitate changes and reflections:

1. Organise the room with four clearly defined positions in place and label them as – first position – second position – third position – and neutral position. You can add a sticker to each spot.

2. Stand over the neutral position and think about a situation where you would like to be more empathic with someone – ready? You have the situation and context in your mind? Good.

3. Now physically move to your first position. This first position is about *your perspective*, and looking at the situation through your own eyes. As you look at the situation from this first position note what you think is relevant or interesting.

4. Once this is done, step out of it and go back to your starting position – the neutral position. Take a few deep breaths in the neutral position.

5. Now move to the second position. This second position is about imagining *how the situation is if you were the other person*. As you physically move to stand over this second position, step into the shoes of the other person, and look at the situation as if you were this person, seeing everything from their own eyes. Note everything relevant that is coming to mind.

6. Once this is done, step out of it and go back to your starting position – the neutral position, and again take a few deep breaths.

7. Next, physically move to the third position, the *independent or the observer* position. As you do so, step into the mind of a detached observer, like someone passing by, and observe the situation as if you were seeing everything for the first time, not knowing either of the protagonists. Note anything relevant.

8. Finally, go back into the neutral position. Take a few more deep breaths. Then compile all the information collected through each of the positions as you take some longer breaths.

At times you may play around with just one perspective, and that's fine. The important point is to always start from the neutral position. When going into that neutral position, ideally step into your self-leadership default posture (Swim 16, and chapter 3, the survival kit).

A moment of reflection in the aquarium

We have built up emotional intelligence as we have gone along, learning from our experiences with courage. Let's enjoy a moment of reflection in the Aquarium with three easy questions:

1) My Favourite Swims in this chapter

2) What I learned about emotional intelligence with these seven Swims

3) Which Swims I would really like to explore further

Congratulations!

You reached self-leadership level 2

Level 1
You know you have innate ability in self-leadership
You have unpacked seven myths giving you more ability in self-leadership
You have your survival kit, and with it seven habits of self-leadership

And NOW Level 2
You've explored seven perspectives of a dynamic self, always in evolution
You have discovered seven elements to emotions
You have practiced seven dives into the river from flexibility to inspiration
You regularly apply your seven habits to partner up with yourself
You unpacked seven skills to EI, aka Emotional Intelligence

9, Swimming through Rough Waters

Usually, what we most fear doing is what we most need to do. As I have heard said, a person's success in life can usually be measured by the number of uncomfortable conversations he or she is willing to have. Resolve to do one thing every day that you fear.

— Timothy Ferriss

Fish to fish

Life is rarely a follow on of easy swims. At least, if it is for you, you are either an exception or a miracle. And the fun of life may be about more than just plain sailing. We are kept on our toes, with our curiosity up and running.

What does that mean, therefore, in terms of self-leadership? That we develop a capability to swim in whatever the water around us is doing, whether it is quiet or rough water. And when the waters get rough, self-leadership is about:

1. Maintaining stability in our comprehension of *who we are* and *what we can do*.
2. Applying flexibility to keep driving *who we are* to *where we want to go*: these famous horizons we have identified.
3. And lastly, maintaining this *where we want to* go as a focus, like a compass.

All three steps happen at the same time, especially when waters get really rough. Still we need to establish step 1 just a bit before the other two, so that we can use it like a very solid buoy to support us. It will give us the clarity of mind we need to apply steps 2 and 3.

We are going to work at it using every swim in this chapter, building up on already acquired skills to develop: resilience, focus and determination, reflection and fast learning, balance and stability, capability to remain in the present, and the vision of our next steps.

When do you know the waters are getting rough?

When you are faced with any situations that may unsettle you or create extra challenges.

It can be: running challenging negotiations, receiving bad news, facilitating difficult meetings, joining in-real-life social networks, handling situations triggering strong emotional reactions, facing a career change, and so on. YOU name it. This chapter is for any type of water YOU may find rough.

Swim 57: Use your survival kit

Our survival kit is as much a survival kit as a first-aid kit. And you want to turn these seven habits into a foundation which has the power to move you away from an immediate emotional reaction onto a delayed chosen reaction. Yes, the seven habits of our survival kit are here to foster stepping back and engaging critical thinking by keeping us calm and centred.

1. **Breathe and drink.** Not only does this ensure full oxygenation of your brain, it helps to maintain a relaxed body and mind, and forces you to pause; the first process to being able to step back.
2. **Take your default posture.** It brings you back into the moment and gives you an actual physical anchor to support you.
3. **Maintain awareness.** Observe everything around you, your environment and the situation. Getting factual information is our second point to being able to step back.
4. **Stay relaxed.** Using breathing and your default posture, focus on keeping everything relaxed. Purposely make slower gestures, telling your body "I'm in charge", which gives you time to think.
5. **Acknowledge your emotion.** Log into your mind the message the emotion is sending, and quickly look for its positive intention. This is our third stage to stepping back; we keep our focus on positive intentions and finding solutions.
6. **Maintain movement.** Having stepped back and moved away from emotional reactions, we can choose an action. When we maintain movement, we maintain control over some outcomes.
7. **Partner up.** Be your best partner.

Tip and Practice, Swim 57:

The Tip! The seven habits of our survival kit are here to foster stepping back and engaging critical thinking by keeping us calm and centred. When we apply them we move away from an emotional reaction into a delayed chosen reaction.

The Practice! Daily, in any type of situation, take a moment to review the seven habits of your survival kit and focus on applying each, one by one. Repeat this exercise as often as you can to turn them into a reflex action.

Swim 58: Leave thinking aside

It's another morning, neither bright nor sunny, and you are looking through the window searching for something precise. In your head you can hear the words, "I need to understand", like a mantra, "If I understand I can decide. If I understand I can act". But you stay there, searching further into your head, further down into the rabbit hole and the analytical world.

The reality of the moment? You are probably chasing your own tail. You have surely seen videos of cats or dogs turning in circles, chasing their own tails. This is exactly what we do when we are looking for understanding. We go over and over the same rational arguments, the same information, stopping the flow of actions and, with it, movement. Still, we know movement is everywhere and everything is movement. A thought, like a memory, is a movement; a chemical and electrical signal, sent from one region of the brain to another along a neural pathway.

To avoid chasing our own tail, we have to learn to leave thinking aside.

To do that we focus on creating movement. We often start with the creation of a physical movement, which leads to a simple change of context, or breaks a pattern. It also gives us back some ownership over a situation. And yes, the action will trigger the understanding we are looking for. However, rather than seeking it at the beginning, we are going to receive it later on.

Tip and Practice, Swim 58:

The Tip! Learn to leave thinking aside and focus on creating movement. A simple physical movement is often enough to break patterns, and yes even the decision to go for a sleep can be seen as a physical movement.

The Practice! Let's start with an easy-to-use technique of brainstorming in three stages:

1. Write a question you have been thinking of on a piece of paper and jot down answers and ideas as they come up spontaneously.
2. Once done, leave the paper on the table and go for a ten to fifteen minute walk; if possible walk outdoors and daydream.
3. Come back to your paper and, for another ten to fifteen minutes, dig deeper looking for more ideas. Repeat stage 2 and 3 if necessary.[29]

Swim 59: Apply the three Fs of learnings

Okay, the water is rough, your stomach is a bit up and down as you swim there, and still you want to learn something from the experience. Only then you know you will have added the skills you need to ensure two things; firstly, you will not repeat the same situation, and secondly, you are strengthening your self-leadership as you swim along.

There are two types of learning; a positive learning or a negative learning. A negative learning is something like "I don't want to do that any longer", and it tells you nothing about the skills you may need to ensure that. A positive learning is something like "From now on, I want to do this ...", and it gives us an idea about either a skill or a direction to focus on. We can, in fact, link this to our Swim 47: Practice focus.

A positive learning is usually stated in an *affirmative* sentence, written in the *present* tense and includes *"I"* as the subject. I use the acronym API as an easy mnemonic.

Let's now review the three "Fs" of positive learning:

1. *F for fail*. A situation did not go as smoothly as expected and the results are not what you wanted. That's okay; FAIL can be read as *First Attempt In Learning*. Acknowledge the situation and pause.
2. *F for feedbacks*. Using this one question, "What is important (for me) to learn from this experience?" Note every answer that comes to mind until you can phrase it as an API sentence or several sentences.
3. *F for future steps*. Using this second question, "What steps am I going to implement to follow up on the API sentences I created within step 2?" Identify actions to take to develop your skills.

With these three Fs to a positive learning, we are developing our growth mindset: our capability to change and our self-directed neuroplasticity.

Tip and Practice, Swim 59:

The Tip! A positive learning is always stated as an API sentence: affirmative, written in the present tense, with "I" as the subject.

The Practice! Take a moment to review experiences you have had lately. Apply the three Fs of positive learnings and reflect on each step, especially step 2. Note in detail what you want to develop with step 3.

Swim 60: Practice stability

The same way we learnt to practice focus in Swim 47, by saying things the way we want them, we are now going to learn to practice *stability*. Like this, when everything is spinning around us, moving at high speed, we will have something solid we can anchor ourselves to. See stability like a buoy which will keep your head above the water; and this buoy is you, the knowledge of who you are, what you can do, and your trust in it.

How do we practice *stability*? Very methodically, using our body and following a five-step process:

1. Using your body, bring back your default posture from Swim 16. If needed, bring to mind the metaphor linked to this posture.
2. Focus on the sensations and impressions you are creating, especially the impressions of strength, firmness, and stability associated with this default posture. Lock it into your mind. I often make a finger snapping sound, but you can find your own mechanism.
3. Identify a repetitive sentence to describe what you are looking to achieve, saying things the way you want them. One of mine is "I practice emotional and physical stability every moment of the day".
4. Repeat step 1 to 3, several times a day for seven days or more, until you know you can recall it any time, like a good habit.
5. If in doubt, always go back to your body and its connection to the ground to re-anchor stability in factual pieces of information.

Stability is in fact a new mental state we are adding to our library of mental states (Swim 52).

Tip and Practice, Swim 60:

The Tip! To practice stability is to practice a strong trust and belief in the knowledge of who we are, what we can do and where we want to go. This knowledge is independent of context and situations, and acts like a buoy we can anchor ourselves to.

The Practice! Practice the five-step process above daily until you have integrated the sequence as a habit, and you can recall the mental state of stability any time you want.

Swim 61: Look for facts

With the last step of our Swim 60 five-step process, we read, "If in doubt, always go back to your body and its connection to the ground to re-anchor stability in factual pieces of information".

Our brain is a funny tool. It does not see what is really there, it sees what it expects to see based on our knowledge, past experiences and expectations. When looking at the actual sense of vision, optical illusions are possible because our brain predicts what to see. And somehow, what we see is what we project, the same way that what we project is what we see. Confusing, right? To refresh your knowledge, you can revisit Swims 22, 23, 27, and 39.

Factual information connects us to what is really happening and helps us to see all the information available. Looking for facts is about leaving the interpretation of a situation aside and instead focusing on what is really happening and therefore what actions can actually be created.

We facilitate that with four actions:

1. Bring yourself back into the moment (Swim 16, 57, or 60 steps 1&5).
2. Pause and take regular deep breaths to force your mind to slow down.
3. Read the situation looking only for facts and factual information. Do challenge your assumptions in order to recover missing information.
4. Replace the word "Why" with "What is important about the situation?" "Why" makes you look for rational, while "What" makes your look for facts.

Tip and Practice, Swim 61:

The Tip! Looking for facts and factual information is about leaving the interpretation of a situation aside and challenging our assumptions. It takes the personal out of the equation and strengthens our trust in ourselves; an amazing side-effect of developing self-leadership.

The Practice! Revisit situations you've experienced recently and reread them looking only for factual information. Take a moment to note in your notebook every fact you can remember. Make sure you split the facts from interpretation. What new choices in your reactions can you see now? Make a list of them. They may be handy next time you come across similar situations.

Swim 62: Practice reframing

Our brain is indeed a funny tool. It enjoys taking shortcuts and filtering our experiences against an existing database of information built up on past events. Taking those shortcuts is how we can think fast. It's also how we can do everything on a daily basis. This in-brain database of information is in fact a collection of references which frame our experiences, and some of these frames are complex schema of unquestioned values and beliefs. Take optimistic people; they tend to see everything through a positive frame, while pessimistic people tend to do the opposite.

To reframe is to decide to look at a situation using a different frame. When we do that, we are challenging our immediate assumptions and our expectations. Let's explore several useful frames:

1. **Meaning** – what else could the situation or behaviour mean?
2. **Context** – where or when could this behaviour or situation be useful?
3. **Positive learning** – what positive information can I learn from this?
4. **Humour** – what is funny about this?
5. **Solution** – what would I be doing if I had solved the problem? Could I do that right now?
6. **Opportunity** – what opportunities are within this situation or experience?
7. **As if** – question the situation as if your desired outcome has been met.
8. **Super Hero** – what would one of my superheroes think? How would they look at, or approach, this situation or experience?

Tip and Practice, Swim 62:

The Tip! To reframe is to decide to look at a situation using a different frame. When we reframe, we open the doors to new ideas and choices. We practice reframing by asking questions.

The Practice! Let's go back to situations you have identified with our Swim 61. And take a moment to assess what spontaneous frame defined each situation. Now, revisit each situation using the eight frames listed above. Ask you read each question, one by one, note every answer in your notebook. Next, identify all the new choices in your reactions you have now available. How could you use this knowledge in the coming days? Clearly document your ideas and comments in your notebook.

Swim 63: Keep an eye on the horizon

Looking at the horizon is about identifying something ahead of us which can give energy and direction to the movements we create (Swim 40). Keeping an eye on this horizon is about maintaining motivation and movement towards it. We can define two types of horizons:

1. **Short-term horizons** – they are goals and objectives typically associated with precise activities and a timeline. For instance, I pass a certification by this date; I write a book by that date, etc.
2. **Long-term horizons** – they are more like intentions – sometimes unprecise – associated with a sense of direction or purpose. They are smooth and fluid; not really linked to any precise timeline. For instance, I want to make a difference for the better; I want to assist people to feel happier, etc.

Our long-term horizons kind of drive the swim. Our short-terms horizons are like stopovers on the way. Ideally, since they serve two different purposes, you should have elements of both always on your mind.

To define your horizons, you start with Swim 40. Focusing on a physical horizon we remind our brain it can look ahead. Then, using our Swim 47: Practice focus, we describe our horizons *the way we want them* with a well-formed API sentence (Affirmative, Positive, with "I"). Next, we associate an image in our mind with our horizons, always leveraging from the API sentence (Swim 53).

To keep an eye on our horizons, regularly bring this image to mind, and repeat your API sentences.

Tip and Practice, Swim 63:

The Tip! When we keep an eye on our horizons, we maintain motivation and movement in our desired direction; and we strengthen determination, willpower and persistence.

The Practice! Let's start with a game using our whole brain as in Swim 48. Take a pen and a paper – your notebook or an independent blank page – and draw whatever comes to mind when you read the following questions one by one: "My horizons are like what?" and "If I knew my horizons, what would they be?"

Some extra swimming for the highly motivated

Feel like swimming further with some added practice? Enjoy!

Extra Practice on Swim 60, practice stability, using our body – We know we have a body (Swim 4), but what if that body is all over the place – Picasso's cubism style – head in clouds, mind in fog, and body lost to the wild, unable to feel what happens around you. When this happens, we need an easy way to bring body and mind back together:

1. Breathe in, breathe out, and grab your bottle of water.
2. Then look at your two feet and the floor you are standing on, or you could be sitting on a chair looking at your feet on the floor.
3. Maybe look at your hands, sitting deeper into a chair, pushing your back against it and your feet onto the ground.
4. Search for factual sensory information linked to your physical body. Is the chair hard? Is the floor soft? Are my feet pushing onto the floor?
5. Use your breath to connect with your chest and stomach. Take a deep breath and focus on seeing your belly move, or your chest opening, exhaling tension as you breathe out, chest up and relax.
6. Maybe visualise a tree; your feet like roots into the ground.
7. Or maybe see a heavy rock; strong and robust against flooding water.
8. Step by step, become part of the room anchoring your stability on physical elements. Focus on the room and everything happening in the room; notice how you are becoming part of it.

With this short routine, you ground yourself in the moment, in time and space, and you allow your brain to access existing resources.

Extra Practice on Swim 63, keeping an eye on the horizon – Looking at the drawings you've done, know that their style and content are always the right one for you. Study them one by one, and quickly note every word coming into your head. Once done, take your non-writing hand, and write some of the key words slowly.

Now go for a short walk and daydream.

Next, using the words you listed, write several API sentences to comment on each drawing. Take your time. Identify short versus long term horizons. And, link your short-term ones to dates.

A moment of reflection in the aquarium

Seven more Swims completed and not just any type of Swims: Swims to make it through rough water. Let's step back with three easy questions:

1) My Favourite Swims in this chapter

2) The Practice Swims I have already implemented as habits

3) The Swims which inspired me to dive further

10, Your Brain and You

The systemic training of the mind, the cultivation of happiness, the genuine inner transformation by deliberating, selecting and focusing on positive mental states and challenging negative mental states, is possible because of the very structure and function of the brain. But the wiring of our brains is not static, not irrevocably fixed. Our brains are also adaptable.

– Dalai Lama & Howard Cutler

Fish to fish

When the water gets rough, we apply self-leadership focusing on three things.

We maintain stability in our comprehension of *who we are* and *what we can do*. Then, we apply flexibility to keep driving *who we are* to *where we want to go*; these famous horizons we have identified. And lastly, we keep an eye on *where we want to go*, using our horizons like compasses.

We can easily see how self-leadership builds on strengthening already acquired skills; such as resilience, determination, reflection, fast learning, balance, stability, capability to remain in the present, vision, observation, capability to step back, willpower, creativity, etc.

All those skills have one huge thing in common: they all depend on a very healthy brain able to work at its best. And to keep your brain healthy and able to work at its best, you need to know a minimum of its processes and habits.

Let's explore how our brain works and what it needs.

Swim 64: Two Instagram feeds

Our brain speaks two languages: a rational and a visual or symbolic one (Swim 48). But our brain's native language is the visual one; and our brain records everything – what has happened and what may come next – as images. You can imagine this as two simultaneous Instagram feeds: one tracking past and current experiences, one predicting future experiences. With a minor addition: both feeds are extremely dynamic.

While your smartphone Instagram story is stable, a picture remaining as it is once posted; the Instagram feeds in your brain are recreated every time, and pictures change and evolve as time goes by.

For past experiences, this is linked to memories being dynamic processes. In fact, a memory is a reconstruction of the experience of the moment based on what we filtered and recorded with our senses (visual, audio, kinaesthetic, olfactory, gustatory – and other senses' information[30]). After consolidation, long-term memories are stored throughout the brain as groups of neurons that are primed to fire together in the same pattern that created the original experience, and each component of a memory is stored in the brain area that initiated it (e.g. groups of neurons in the visual cortex store as sight, neurons in the amygdala store the associated emotion, etc.)[31].

A projection in our future follows the same process. It is a construction of the experiences we expect using the same neurological processes approach.

Tip and Practice, Swim 64:

The Tip! Memories, learnings and future experiences, are stored as images in our brain. When we remember something, we bring back the image by activating neural pathways to recreate the experience. Changing the neural pathway can therefore modify the experience and its meaning.

The Practice! Think about something which is always true for you. When you think about that do you have a picture in mind? Is it black and white or in colour? Is the picture near or far versus your own body? Can you identify other sensory details associated with that picture? Note them in your note book. Repeat the exercise thinking about something which is always false for you.

What differences do you see in how you coded the two images?

Swim 65: A high-level athlete

Your brain is like a high-level athlete participating in the Olympics and international competitions; often swimming a marathon swim on a daily basis. And like any high-level athlete, your brain needs three things to keep up and carry on collecting those gold medals:

1. Regular exercise to keep muscles in shape or develop new ones.
2. Regular energy input.
3. Regular quality rest periods.

What I call *brain muscles* is a metaphor for *neural process*, *neural pathways* or any process of neurons activation. And yes, we already developed brain muscles with our Swim 36 and the training of our *change muscle*. Indeed, strengthening a neural pathway is like strengthening a muscle; it is done through repetition and practice. To create a *balanced brain*, as we do when creating a *balanced body*, we practice different muscles with different exercises.

We need energy to fuel these brain muscles; 20 to 25% of all the energy we produce. And to create a *power brain*, as we do when creating a *power body*, we feed it with good and diverse food.

And lastly the rest periods. An exhausted athlete cannot perform. An exhausted brain runs crazy. We use two types of resting periods, sleeping and day-dreaming – the latter we can do while walking or physically exercising.

Tip and Practice, Swim 65:

The Tip! Your brain is a high level athlete and, like any high level athlete, it needs three things to function at its best: regular exercises, regular energy input, and regular quality rest periods.

The Practice! We start with a short assessment. Answer each of the following questions in your notebook. How many resting periods do you take in a regular working day? How often do you alternate intense brain concentration and day-dreaming or physical exercise? How regular is your sleeping pattern, e.g., the time you go to bed, the time you wake up? How often do you eat in a day? How healthy do you think is your diet? What brain muscles are you training right now?

Swim 66: A careful use of energy

Our brain consumes 20 to 25% of all the energy we produce. Still this energy is not unlimited and cannot feed all the parts of our brain at the same time. We want to choose where we burn this energy.

Take your pre-frontal cortex for instance. It is located at the front of your brain, just behind your forehead and activates when you use the following skills: willpower, decision-making, self-control, big picture thinking, emotional intelligence, complicated reasoning, creativity, etc. If you are to activate all these at the same time, each skill will compete with the others for energy, and some will deprive others of the needed energy.

Let's say you have to work on a very time-constrained project, asking for fast thinking and decision making. At the same time you decide to train for a marathon and also start a diet. These four actions will compete for energy within your brain, and you may struggle to keep fuelling all of them.

Choose where you burn your brain energy. Assess the tasks you have running and objectively review if the skills needed to complete them may compete with each other.

Pay also attention to *overstimulating a neural pathway* without giving it time to rest and clean. This can as well impact its capability in correctly functioning.

Tip and Practice, Swim 66:

The Tip! Your brain has access to a limited amount of energy. Choose wisely how you use your brain energy.

The Practice! Take your notebook and on a blank page list the skills you are using daily. It can be: will-power, resilience, determination, planning, time management, self-control, creativity, focus, attention to detail, big picture thinking, etc.

Now assess how balanced your brain feels, where 0 will be really poor and 10 is amazing and great. And next, going through each skill, rate how much energy you are spending on it.

Go for a 30 minute walk. Once back, look at your ratings. Any comments?

Swim 67: A fanatical student

Not only is our brain a high-level athlete, it is a fanatical student. Always up and ready for some learning, it will never leave grey or white matter unused. Before we reached 7-8 years old, the brain is like a sponge, it absorbs everything as possible learning; and then we refine, select areas to develop, bring in new information, develop neural pathways, and so on.

There are several cool points to know about our brain and learning:

1. Learning changes the physical structure of the brain.
2. These changes alter the functioning of our brain. Learning organises and reorganises our brain; which we describe as neuroplasticity.
3. Different parts of the brain are ready to learn at different times.
4. Learning combines two systems; one based on *declarative learning* such as explicit reasoning, listening to a lecture, etc. and one focusing on *procedural learning* sometimes called muscle memory. When we learn a task such as identifying wines, we use both systems.
5. Learning can be passive or active.

Our brain is designed for learning. Choose what you are learning about, and actively train your **learning muscle** to keep it sharp and strong, so that you can develop self-directed neuroplasticity.

Tip and Practice, Swim 67:

The Tip! Our brain is designed for learning, and it uses learning to organise and reorganise itself (neuroplasticity). When we actively choose what to learn, we can practice self-directed neuroplasticity.

The Practice! What are you learning at the moment? Start with this question: what skills am I learning right now?" Do list everything, from the skills you are learning in your leisure time to the ones you are learning at work.

Next, answer this question: what skills am I passively learning right now? For that, use a three step process. 1. List what has happened during your day. 2. Reflect on the experiences to identify lessons learned. 3. Check and confirm this is actually something you want to learn (Swim 59).

Looking at both lists choose three to five skills to focus on.

Swim 68: A multilingual approach

Our brain's native language is not only a visual one, it is a language based on our senses; and it uses music, movements, sensations, images and symbols. When listening to music, both audio and motor cortex-areas activate getting most of us ready to jump and dance; and if it was not for this idea of self-consciousness, we would all stand up and dance. When we use active imagination, we let the native storyteller in us speak; when we go to a movie, watching superheroes flying, we suspend our disbelief and let the native dreamer in us speak.

Our brain has also learned a rational language using words, and for more than three centuries now, western societies have leveraged a lot from sciences and reasons.

Is that all? Of course not, we can challenge our thinking, and agree that our brain speaks many more languages referring to the nine types of intelligence we described in chapter 8: body smart, picture smart, nature smart, sound smart, word smart, rational smart, self-smart, people smart, or life smart.

So what is important about the above? It's not the many brain languages we could define, but the fact that our brain works in many different ways, using lots of different mechanisms and processes. The more we leverage from all these different mechanisms, the more brain power we use.

Tip and Practice, Swim 68:

The Tip! By using all aspects of our brain, all its natural languages and natural capabilities, we are increasing our possibilities and our self-leadership.

The Practice! Today, to strengthen creativity and flexibility, let's focus on less-used languages. Take a pen, a blank page, and draw. Let your hand draw without looking for perfect pictures. Swap between your writing hand and the other. Now, put some music on, and let your feet move. Forget about rhythm or beat, just let your feet move and let your mind go with it. What about exploring juggling? Find three balls; look for a crash course on YouTube, and go. Next singing? The music is still on, have your own little karaoke in your living room, and let your voice take over.

Swim 69: A connected body

Our brain is attached to a body. More precisely our brain is located under our skull and this skull is attached to a skeleton. The skeleton is wrapped in muscles and skin, and within the skeleton we have organs, blood, hormones, chemicals, as well as many systems like: nervous systems, immune systems, and endocrine systems; and these systems regulate hormones, heart rate, blood pressure, etc. Our brain's frontal lobes, amygdala and hippocampus are actually extensively connected with these immune, endocrine and nervous systems and we have a fascinating two-way feedback loop. Our mental state influences our physical state and our physical state influences our mental state. Our body is much more than just a body. Our body can really be an instrument of strong mental state development and self-leadership. For instance:

- **To clear your mind** – physically clear space around you.
- **To feel bigger and more visible** – make your body bigger and breathe bigger.
- **To feel stable** – make your body as strong as a rock.
- **To strengthen persistence and determination skills** – practice a long distance type of sport, like running, cycling, cross-county skating, etc.
- **To feel flexible in your mind** – develop a flexible body – and it starts with a simple daily stretch.
- **To calm down** – chew slowly, breathe slowly, write slowly, move slowly, speak slowly, etc.

Project with your body what you want to project with your mind: a robust body for a robust mind; a smiling body for an open mind; an assertive body happy to make physical space for an assertive mind.

Tip and Practice, Swim 69:

The Tip! Our body is much more than just a body. Project with your body what you want to project with your mind and use the strength of your body to strengthen your desired mental state.

The Practice! Go back to the library of mental states you are building (see our Swim 52). For each mental state, note how you could use your body to add another layer of strength. If you are unsure how to start, revisit our Swim 12, and the work of Amy Cuddy for inspiration. Next, leveraging from the work on the default posture (see survival kit) further develop your mental states, adding your body strength.

Swim 70: A trio (or more?)

An octopus is said to have nine brains; a central one and ganglions at the end of each arm with the capability to touch and recognise. A human is said to have three, though we may discover more as research progress.

First, we have our big brain hidden within our skull; it has two hemispheres, mapped in several cortices, and is connected by the corpus callosum.

Next, we have a gut-brain. It is hidden within our gut, and made of neural tissue filled with important neurotransmitters and a network of neurons. This gut-brain is equipped with its own reflexes and senses, and is able to behave independently of the head-brain. It carries information from the gut-brain to the head-brain, with the capability to influence our mental state. What if *having a gut feeling* is simply our gut-brain giving us information? What if *having butterflies in our stomach* means our gut-brain is reading the situation for us?

And lastly we talked about a heart-brain. It is a complex intrinsic nervous system of several types of neurons, neurotransmitters and support cells, located in the heart, independent from the head-brain and able to send it messages. For instance the heart-brain can send information directly to the amygdala, where the amygdala is a key centre in processing emotions.

Tip and Practice, Swim 70:

The Tip! We are talking about three brains: our head-brain, our gut-brain, and our heart-brain. All brains can talk with each other, and at times the gut-brain and heart-brain actually inform or give direction to our head-brain.

The Practice! Let's build up on observation, adding two more layers to self-awareness. What is your gut telling you today? What is your heart saying? Ok. This practice may sound surprising but still go with it. Ask your gut "What do you want to tell me today?" and note in your notebook whatever comes into your head. Repeat the same question with your heart.

Link this information to our previous Swim 59, and reflect on how having three brains strengthens this notion of connected body.

Some extra swimming for the highly motivated

Feel like swimming further with some added practice? Enjoy!

Extra practice on our Swim 67, a fanatical student – We can facilitate learning by creating the right context or environment, and here are nine tips to do so:

1. Stay relaxed.
2. Focus – five minutes focus is better than 20 minutes multitasking.
3. Teach others.
4. Actively engage with your learning.
5. Include an emotional base.
6. Challenge yourself.
7. Pat yourself for the effort, more than for the result.
8. Think short sessions but often.
9. Enjoy it.

Extra practice on our Swim 69, a connected body – Your body is an incredible tool and instrument you can use to strengthen your mental state; such a strong instrument that people working on the phone all day will still have classes on how to use their body when talking on the phone. Simple, your body posture impacts the mechanics of your vocal chords and therefore the quality of your voice.

Bodies are designed with very specific mechanics and equilibrium; and when one element goes off balance, everything else can be impacted. A good source of information to explore would be the documented methodology from the "Alexander Technique" which will echo our Swim 18; staying relaxed.

Also body movement can act as a *pattern interrupt*. If a situation gets out of hand, a gesture as simple as chewing slowly or taking a sip of water has an immediate effect by creating a break in the moment or a pattern interrupt, bringing our focus away from the situation to an actual action.

In addition to balance and mechanics, the actual use of our body generates hormones, and these do impact our mental states as well as how people may perceive us (Swim 12).

A moment of reflection in the aquarium

Seven more Swims completed, and now a better understanding on how our brain works, and how we can influence it. Time to reflect:

1) My Favourite Swims in this chapter

2) How am I going to look after my brain?

3) What did I like knowing about the brain?

11, Swimming through Muddy Waters

Self-discipline is – A skill that can be learned – Becoming aware of your subconscious resistances to action, then overcoming those resistances – The process of coordinating your conscious and subconscious psychological elements.

– Theodore Bryant

Fish to fish

When the water gets rough, we focus in trusting the knowledge we have of *who we are* and *what we can do;* and we use this knowledge like a solid buoy to support us.

What to do when the waters get muddy?

Can the water actually get muddy?

What if they were always muddy?

In the context of self-leadership, the quality of the water does not change much to the story. Being muddy waters, quiet waters, rough waters; these are simply different paradigms within which we swim. And each paradigm will call for different set of skills.

What matters is how long we swim, and in which direction. And for that we go back to the three steps we started exploring in chapter 9:

1. We maintain stability in our comprehension of *who we are* and *what we can do*.
2. We apply flexibility to keep moving *where we want to go*: these famous horizons we have identified.
3. We keep these horizons a main focus, like a heading on a compass.

With this final chapter, we are going to explore tools and philosophy behind the world of self-leadership, especially interesting to use when the waters get muddy. But first, what are muddy waters?

Swim 71: A new paradigm

The word *paradigm* has a nice ring to it. It is defined as a "philosophical or theoretical framework of any kind, something similar to a model or a system." The way we comprehend life around us is usually defined by combining paradigms. Our aquariums are also organised around paradigms.

One of the oldest ways of construing our realities and universe has been to organise them as pairs of opposites – night and day – sun and moon – man and woman – black and white – good and evil – art and science – reason and emotion – mind and body – left and right brain, etc. We even read at times about the dichotomy of nature[32], or its binary aspects. This is a paradigm in itself and with it comes a huge limitation; you are either one or the other, and never a combination of both.

What about the dichotomy of mind and body? Here again we acknowledge today that, as human beings, we are neither one nor the other, but a clever combination of body and mind in constant communication. What about our brain? Correct, we have right and left hemispheres, and still research shows cognitive processes involve an intrinsic collaboration between the two hemispheres without the clear cut that was initially thought.

Welcome to the muddy waters paradigm where elements are neither black nor white but dynamic, continuously evolving through shades of grey.

Tip and Practice, Swim 71:

The Tip! The muddy waters paradigm is a framework of thinking, where we accept the assumption that nothing is black or white, but continuously evolving shades of grey. In such a paradigm, paradoxes exist and are acceptable; the same way that agreeing to disagree becomes a regular possibility.

The Practice! Take a deep breath and look back to past situations or experiences where you may have reacted in a paradigm of dichotomy. Someone was right or wrong; the story was black or white; the behaviour was good or bad, etc. Look at those same situations now through the muddy waters paradigm. What can you see now? What is changing as you re-assess the situations?

Swim 72: A tool for learning

While reading this book you have been using an incredible tool for learning. As you developed your self-leadership, every step on the way, in fact at every single page, I've asked you to pause, to ask yourselves questions and to note your answers.

I've asked you to practise self-reflection.

Self-reflection is our capacity and willingness to learn more about our fundamental nature. With self-leadership we use this capability to learn more about *who we are*, *what we can do* and *where we want to go* in order to improve our skills and ourselves.

One word of caution though: for self-reflection to remain a useful tool for learning, you want to keep it an interesting and fun activity to do. If it becomes an obsession, take a break and forget about it for a while. For that, go straight back to our survival kit, and habit sixth maintain movement.

Tip and Practice, Swim 72:

The Tip! When developing self-leadership we use self-reflection as a tool to identify skills to develop and competencies to reach; always focusing on the positive learnings we gain through our experiences. As your self-leadership increases so is your capability to self-reflect; to a point that you want self-reflection to become a habit.

The Practice! Every day, find a moment to step back. Ideally in the evening, as your day comes to an end. Use our Swim 59, as a several steps approach to self-reflection.

Four constructive tips when practising self-reflection:

1. Replace any *Why* questions with a lot of *What* and *How* questions. For instance, "Why should I do that?" becomes "What is important to me about doing that?"
2. Check regularly, at least once a week, that you are doing something which brings you one step closer to your objectives and horizons.
3. Remember that changing can be a smooth and easy action.
4. Ensure that you draw, sing, dance, write, talk and have fun partnering with yourself.

Swim 73: A power tool

Who would have thought that two words, as simple as *"what"*, an undefined or neutral word, and *"if"*, a conjunction, could combine in such an impactful and interesting question? A question so interesting that we can even find a Wikipedia entry on it, and be surprised to discover many articles, movies, albums or songs proudly starring ***What if*** in their title.

What if provides us with a provocative hypothetical question which gives us permission to explore the impossible so that we can make it possible. "What if we could fly?" The first time someone asked this question it was impossible, but nowadays it is. *What if* questions break the paradigm we are usually working within and create a change of perspective. They have a similar effect as the *As if* frame (Swim 62), however with a wider scope.

When it comes to developing self-leadership, a *what if* question is a very powerful tool which suspends our disbelief in situations or in the person we are, so that we can identify solutions and swim in unknown waters.

- ***What if*** I could learn that?
- ***What if*** I could react this way easily?
- ***What if*** I could change naturally?
- ***What if*** I could trust to always know how to react?
- ***What if*** I had already found a solution?
- ***What if*** I could find the time to learn something new?
- ***What if*** I could easily manage my emotions?
- ***What if*** I was already a great self-leader?

Tip and Practice, Swim 73:

The Tip! Asking *what if* cracks the windows of our aquarium so that we can start swimming in rivers and oceans.

The Practice! Take a moment to read again the *what if* questions given above. Then, on a big piece of paper write WHAT IF in capital letters. Now, think about a situation challenging you at the moment. Going back to the piece of paper, as you read WHAT IF, write all the *what if* questions you would like to apply to this situation. Pause for a moment.

Going back to your paper, select the *what if* question you want to start with to design new solutions to the situation.

Swim 74: A few pillars and an invitation

What if we were to define four pillars of self-leadership? They could be elements, precise elements of self-leadership; or they could be principles, i.e. defining a framework of thought or philosophy to follow; or they could be part of our definition. For example:

Four pillars as *elements of self-leadership*:

1. Awareness – full awareness: us, others, the system.
2. Growth mindset – our attitude towards failure.
3. Flexibility – the less we control, the more we control.
4. Humility – unique and all the same.

Four pillars as *principles of self-leadership*:

1. Movement is everything and everything starts with movement.
2. Changes can happen smoothly and step by step.
3. Learning is about widening the size of our comfort zone.
4. Partnering up with oneself is using all our available resources.

Four pillars as *definitions of self-leadership*:

1. Knowing and improving *who we are*.
2. Knowing and expanding *what we can do*.
3. Identifying and refining *where we want to go*.
4. Developing and strengthening *our ability to influence our communication, emotions and behaviours*.

Tip and Practice, Swim 74:

The Tip! By choosing words wisely and saying things the way we want them, we are taking ownership for our understanding and therefore our learnings and experiences. By defining what you see behind the word self-leadership, you take a stronger ownership for your development in self-leadership.

The Practice! Here is your invitation. What if you were to define your own pillars of self-leadership? Take your notebook. Open it at a brand-new, clean page. In BIG LETTERS, write your own four (or more) pillars of self-leadership.

Swim 75: A few words and an action

What skills have we linked to self-leadership so far? Resilience, focus, determination, vision, learning, maintaining balance, stability, calm, centred, grounded, acceptance, comfort zone, exploration, will-power, dissociation, association, congruency, independence, love, respect, curiosity, optimism, reliability, flexibility, confidence, autonomy, self-awareness, humility, motivation, creativity, trust, etc.

All these skills are also words, and they all may mean something slightly different to you than to me; especially the word self-leadership. This comes from two facts: words are labels and not the actual skill or experience; and words are pre-loaded with meaning (Swim 43).

This pre-loaded meaning is based on our societies, environment, and cultures. Give students, from a creative writing course in Ireland, the exercise to write a one-page text starting with the sentence "He appeared". You are likely to see more than 70% of them writing about religion, Christ and priests; another 20-25% about ghosts and spirits; and a small 5% maybe about something like "He appeared with a fresh loaf of bread"[33].

I like to say *"Words are wild beasts! And in life you have two choices; you can either tame them or be their prey"*. How do you tame a word? You turn it into a conscious word (page 39 and keep reading below).

Tip and Practice, Swim 75:

The Tip! To tame a word turn it into a conscious word.

The Practice! Pick several words from the list above. At your own speed, turn each of the selected words into a conscious word. Record these into your notebook. Do the same thing with the following words: SELF-LEADERSHIP, TRUST, I TRUST MYSELF. Ensure to record your conscious words in your notebook. Read them regularly until their definitions are fully committed to your memory.

Note our three easy steps to create a conscious word:
1. Write the word vertically on a page, one letter per line
2. For each letter find a noun or adjective you associate with the word
3. When possible turn the combination of nouns or adjectives into a sentence (optional).

Swim 76: Top 10 tips and one more

ONE – Know your spontaneous breathing rhythm, how to change it, and how to practice cardiac coherence (Survival kit, Swims 15, 18).

TWO – Practice stability with a very strong default posture (Survival kit, Swim 16; then Swim 60) and use your body as a tool (Swim 69).

THREE – Maintain awareness at all times, and practice "being in the moment" (Survival kit, Swim 17; then Swims 22, 23, 34, 38, 50, 51, 52)

FOUR – Explore the world of emotions – anger, fear, impatience, trust, love, empathy, patience, compassion, loving, kindness – and partner with them by listening to their message (Swims 29 to 35; then 50 to 56).

FIVE – Maintain movement and know when to leave thinking aside (Survival kit, Swim 20; then Swims 58, 70, 72).

SIX - Visualise the outcome you want to create, and say it the way you want it (Swims 40, 47, 63).

SEVEN – Always look for positive learnings (Swims 59, 60, 62, 72) and continuously partner-up (Survival kit, Swim 21; then Swims 43 to 49).

EIGHT – Use the power of reframing; especially the power of reframing emotion, feeling, and interpretation (Swims 31 to 34; then Swim 62).

NINE – Be the most flexible element of the system and focus on the horizons (Survival kit, Swim 18, 20; and then Swims 36, 40, 42).

TEN – Bring humour into the picture; and an easy way to bring humour is to start by laughing about ourselves (Survival kit, Swim 21; then Swims 56, 61, 66).

And **ONE MORE** – practice, practice, practice and enjoy!

Tip and Practice, Swim 76:

The Tip! Paradoxes are good fun. One I really like is *the less we control, the more we control*. When we develop flexibility and stop focusing on controlling every single moment, we can direct our attention to controlling outcomes and results.

The Practice! Every day, practice our top 10 tips above until they become habit. Use Swims 21, 59, and 72 to get the most of these tips.

Swim 77: Only the beginning

Self-leadership is having a developed sense of who we are, what we can do, and where we are going, coupled with the ability to influence our communication, emotions and behaviours on the way to getting there.

Through these 77 swims, we explored who we are. One key learning? Who we are is a dynamic notion, which evolves with our physiology, our mood, and our experiences. Swimming comfortably through this flexibility is a strength we develop by practising stability and using our survival kit.

We also explored what we can do and with that we appreciated our innate capability in being an explorer, in creating changes and in learning every single moment. One key learning? Our brain is designed for neuroplasticity, and through self-leadership we create self-directed neuroplasticity, applying a strong growth mindset.

And we explored our ability to influence our communication, emotions and behaviours; with that we confirmed everything is connected, and we are continuously swimming through many interconnected systems such as body-mind-state-behaviour-environment-others, mood-states of mind-emotions-physiology. One key learning? Through self-leadership we connect systems and develop wholesome.

These 77 swims are only the beginning. You have knocked open one wall of your aquarium toward rivers and oceans. Who knows where your swims will take you …

Tip and Practice, Swim 77:

The Tip! This is only the beginning. You have started a spiralling journey, where your skills, capabilities, knowledge and learning will widen daily your spiral toward rivers and oceans.

The Practice! Enjoy the feeling you created by reaching self-leadership levels 1 and 2. Whenever needed, deepen your knowledge by revisiting each swim at leisure and, when ready, move up to the next levels.

A moment of reflection in the aquarium

Our last step-back with three easy questions:

1) What is self-leadership for me?

2) What am I doing every day to enhance my self-leadership?

3) What is important to me about self-leadership?

Congratulations!

On your starting journey to amazing self-leadership

Level 1
You know you have innate ability in self-leadership
You have unpacked seven myths giving you more ability in self-leadership
You have your survival kit, and with it seven habits of self-leadership

Level 2
You've explored seven perspectives of a dynamic self, always in evolution
You have discovered seven elements to emotions
You have practiced seven dives into the river from flexibility to inspiration
You regularly apply your seven habits to partner up with yourself
You unpacked seven skills to EI, aka Emotional Intelligence

And NOW strengthening Level 1 and Level 2
You unpacked seven strength skills to swim through rough waters
You explored how to take maximum benefits from your brain
You discovered waters can get muddy and that's okay

Ready to move up to the next levels

Visit *afishonahill.com* for
More tips and personalised programs

Exceptional leaders distinguish themselves because of superior self-leadership

– Daniel Goleman

Self-leadership doesn't happen by accident. It takes effort, requiring daily practice and attention to make progress.

– S. Jeffrey

Autonomy: the urge to direct our own lives. Mastery: the desire to get better and better at something that matters. Purpose: the yearning to do what we do in the service of something larger than ourselves. These are the building blocks of an entirely new operating system for our businesses.

– Dan Pink

ACKNOWLEDGEMENTS

This book would not exist if it weren't for all the people I was lucky to meet, exchange ideas with, have coaching conversations, and spend evenings talking with, recreating the world and societies. Who we are is closely linked to whom we met, and every person I've met has added something to this book, one way or another.

I thank my parents, my siblings, my nieces and nephews, for seeding in my mind early on the roots of self-leadership and the desire to support and learn from others.

I would like to thank in particular Trevor, Aidan, Kenneth, Bénédicte, Christelle, Frédérique, and Erika for their ongoing support, either reading the first versions of this book, or simply listening to my ongoing reflexion on how to share my thought on self-leadership with others. A huge thank you for Aimee and her fantastic ideas in bringing the book cover to life, and to Sian, my editor, for her support and belief in my own writing style. Without forgetting a huge thank you to the Boreal Café team in Geneva Stand Switzerland who keeps the engine of my mind running thanks to fantastic vanilla lattés.

And thanks to you, the readers, for being curious and spending a moment with me, reading this book.

ABOUT THE AUTHOR

There are two things Florence Dambricourt strongly advocates, the power of self-leadership and the magic of an open mind. Maybe it was her first job, exploring the seas aboard a seismic research boat, which prompted her quest to dive onto the world of self-leadership? Maybe it was rather her experience as an expat, leaving her native land – France – in 1994 to settle in London, then Dublin and lastly in Geneva, Switzerland, which imprinted the importance of having an open mind. Or maybe it was simply the love of the written word, and the publication of *Building Bridges* in 2015, which confirmed her passion for the two subjects, and behind it the power of good communication, emotional intelligence and cognitive behaviourism. Like many coaches, she experiences an extremely strong impulse to assist people in developing and evolving. It drove her to publish *Swim like a fish* and *Speak like a fish*, two books focusing on developing aspect of self-leadership, the human technology of the 21st century. With her dynamic and inspiring keynotes, Florence supports companies to foster culture of innovation, agility and collaboration. Her eyes curious for diversity, novelty and surprising elements, she can often be found hiking through mountains, a notebook, a backpack and two walking poles with her. Do surprise her connecting on afishonahill.com and Social Media and share with her your perspectives on self-leadership and public speaking.

END NOTES

[1] Inspired from Andrew Bryant and Dr. Ana Kazan book published in 2012, *Self-Leadership: how to become a more successful, efficient and effective leader from the inside out.*

[2] An innate ability is a trait or characteristic that is present in an organism at birth. It is always present in the organism and was not a learned behaviour. For example, humans have the innate ability for language – it occurs in all humans naturally. An innate capability can be enhanced through learning evolving through level of competencies.

[3] Maslow's hierarchy of needs (1943) started with 5 levels – Physiological needs (food, water, warmth, rest) – Safety needs (security, safety) – Belongingness and love needs (intimate relationships, friends) – esteem needs (prestige and feeling of accomplishment) – self-actualisation (achieving one's full potential, including creative activities); later in life Maslow added a sixth level – Intrinsic Values. The assumption is that needs lower in the hierarchy must be satisfied before individuals can attend to needs higher up.

[4] Amy Cuddy is a researcher whose research was shared via a TED talk *Your body languages shares who you are* (in October 2018, this TED talk was still listed as one of the top 10 viewed talks) in which she details the effects of "power posing"; more generally she talked about a general phenomenon known as the "postural feedback effect" when taken posture affects hormones creation in the body. For more on the debate over this talk, please read https://ideas.ted.com/inside-the-debate-about-power-posing-a-q-a-with-amy-cuddy/ - for more research on "postural feedback effect" please check the open list maintained by Amy Cuddy's research team at https://docs.google.com/spreadsheets/d/1VZQxTNGncn-x7nz9OsNXmkz9rFkhdYEjzNXN7vqrYKA/pubhtml?gid=1181532305&single=true.

[5] Through research the Hearthmath institute showed cases where the heart was aware of something before the brain, and sending messages to the brain. This is documented through their published book available at https://www.heartmath.org/research/science-of-the-heart/coherence/. For examples on coherence cardiac exercise, simply type "coherence cardiac" on YouTube and enjoy!

[6] For a short description on how a deep breath can impact your heart beat, you may enjoy this post - http://explorecuriocity.org/Explore/ArticleId/705/why-does-your-heart-rate-decrease-when-you-take-a-deep-breath-705.aspx.

[7] On the history of emotions and the building of this new field of research, please refer to the work or Tiffany Watt Smith; you may want to start with a TED talk *The history of human emotions* published in November 2017 at a TED Institute event in Germany. An interesting notion of emotions as a cognitive phenomenon will be

developed later on.

[8] Some fascinating experiences in recovering audio from movement of inanimate objects such as a bag of chips were published by MIT in 2014 - http://news.mit.edu/2014/algorithm-recovers-speech-from-vibrations-0804

[9] Initially the notion of senses was associated to our five primary senses, visual, audio, olfactive, gustatory, and kinaesthetic; then literature like movies used the idea of a sixth sense, a sense of what was paranormal. Nowadays, thanks to progress in research (and therefore a more precise terminology) we talked of a lot more senses, for instance –proprioception –equilibrioception –Kinaesthesia – theroception –Nociception –Chronoception; as well as some senses at the moment only proven (for the moment) in the animal world such as –electroreception – magnetoreception. If interested in exploring more, start by a simple search on the internet "more than five senses."

[10] There are countless number of intranet posts – journalistic reviews or research summary – on the subject of "how much information we receive" and "how much information we are really aware or conscious of." An interesting starting point on that subject would be some research from Gerard Hodgkinson on decision making, and the use of unconscious information in our decision making. Most drivers, extreme sports professionals, or military professionals would have also experienced this type of unconscious awareness; the same one which makes us close our eyes before we realised an object was being sent at us. You can refer to the following article on Forbes as an example for references toward research papers – https://www.forbes.com/sites/daviddisalvo/2013/06/22/your-brain-sees-even-when-you-dont/#747ee302116a.

[11] That's even arguable, since depending on the source quoted; this percentage varies from 0.07% to 0.1%.

[12] As described by Daniel Kahneman in his book *Thinking, Fast and Slow,* the experiencing self is the "you" in the moment, while the remembering self is the "you" who writes the story post the event. To start exploring the subject, you can also start with his TED talk from 2010, *The riddle of experience vs. memory.*

[13] Allan Watts was a British philosopher who interpreted and popularised Eastern philosophy for a Western Audience. This sentence is extracted from talks available on YouTube, especially the one referred to as *Life is not a journey.*

[14] First experiences on the effect of fake smiling were made by Doctor Duchenne, a French Doctor from the nineteenth century, though we had to wait for the work of Dr. Paul Ekman and his team to validate the thought. While doing analysis on the FACS (Faction Action Coding System) where Dr. Ekman's train themselves in practicing facial expressions linked to emotions, they clearly identified a change in their mood, either happy or sad, depending on the emotions being studied. They had to wait for MRI techniques to prove a correlation between taking facial expressions and feeling the relevant emotions (around 1980). Nowadays much

research has strengthened the findings giving us better understanding on how to stimulate the generation of "feel good hormones" such as oxytocin.

[15] Dr Paul Ekman's work was ground breaking in breaking up the assumed correlation culture and emotions. Working with isolated tribes from remote locations, he was able to prove that facial expressions of certain emotions were recognised by all, even though they had not received any influences linked to media or others.

[16] Following a week's dialogue session with the Dalai Lama (see Daniel Goleman, *Destructives Emotions and how we can overcome them*); Dr. Paul Ekman engaged into a new project called "the atlas of emotions" which led to the web site of the same name; where, starting from the six universal emotions he identified, he described derivative emotions; as well as labels in more detail how to recognise one emotion versus another one. Other models exist to describe emotions such Robert Plutchik's model with its wheel of emotions. With this model Plutchik starts with 8 primary emotions, grouped into four pairs of polar opposites – joy & sadness, anger & fear, trust & distrust, surprise & anticipation. Derivative emotions are then created by adding emotions together, for instance, love becomes a combination of joy and trust, guilt a combination of Joy and fear. It is interesting to note that guilt is often said to be a man-made emotion, rather than a natural one. The oldest model on emotions which was found can be traced back to Aristotle, which would be about 350 BC.

[17] Dr. Damasio, A., *Descartes' Error* , page 147, Vintage Edition 2006

[18] The word *emotion* is a tricky one as research across the board does not seem to use it always in the same way. Dr. A. Damasio seems to link emotions to the actual physiological responses, while Dr. Lisa Feldman Barrett seems to use more emotions as the interpretation of the physiological responses. Through her research, Lisa Feldman Barrett points out that there is not a one-to-one response between behaviour and emotion category; in other words, *"stimulation of the same site produces different mental states across instances, depending on the prior state of the individual and also the immediate context."* She concludes that this means there is more going on when a person feels an emotion than just a physiological response: some kind of processing must happen between the physiological response and the perception of the emotion. It seems this kind of processing is what Dr. A Damasio called the feelings; and this is how I used the terminology through this book.

[19] Extracted from the work of Cameron-Bandler and Lebeau, *Emotional Hostage*; interestingly these dimensions echoes some of the assumptions Plutchik made when building its model to describe emotions.

[20] In the movie *Cast Away,* the man character Chuck, while lost on an isolated island, made himself a companion out of a volleyball that he nicknamed Wilson and begin talking to as if it was really another person.

[21] Model of communication inspired from Shannon Claude E. *A mathematical theory of communication.*

[22] The theory starts with the first four steps, also described as the "four steps of learning" or the "four stages of competencies". The addition of the fifth step is inspired from the work of Richard Restak and his definition of expertise (see end note 25).

[23] Restak, R., *The New Brain: How the Modern Age is Rewiring Your Mind*, page 28, Rodale Edition 2004

[24] In his funny TED talk from 2011, *Why you will fail to have a great career*, 2011, Larry Smith plays with the amazing human ability we have to find excuses for everything we do. Go and listen to it, and challenge yourself to find more humour and fun in actually taking ownership for what you do.

[25] NLP stands for Neuro-Linguistic-Programming. It is a field of studies borrowing knowledge from various fields such as psychology, sociology, cognitive behaviourism, linguistics.

[26] The notion of "neutral language" comes from the work of Penny Tompkins and James Lawley on Symbolic Modelling and the Clean Language, Clean Space and Emergent Knowledge processes of David Grove. You can follow their work at the following site https://www.cleanlanguage.co.uk/ For a full list of clean languages question see https://cleanlearning.co.uk/blog/discuss/clean-language-questions.

[27] More can be read from Howard Gardner's most popular book *Frames of Mind: The Theory of Multiple Intelligences.* For a short and well-made infographic why not looking at the work of Mark Vital at https://blog.adioma.com/9-types-of-intelligence-infographic/

[28] Many research can be found on how our brain is cleaning itself of toxins (and more) through the process of sleep; for instance Jeff Iliff TED talk from 2014 *One more reason to get a good night's sleep.* It seems that during sleep, the flow of cerebrospinal fluid increases dramatically, washing away harmful waste proteins that build up between brain cells during waking hours.

[29] Here again many research support the positive impact of physical activities, especially walking, onto cognitive processes; alternating actually thinking and walking has been used as creativity or brainstorming processes. For some examples of reports on creative thinking you can check the two following posts as starting points – https://www.ncbi.nlm.nih.gov/pubmed/24749966 – https://www.apa.org/pubs/journals/releases/xlm-a0036577.pdf

[30] Within the field of NLP, Neuro-Linguistics-Programming, it is assumed that all experiences we are living are stored in our brain as *Internal Representation (or IR),* and these IR are coded with our five primary senses, audio, visual, olfactive, gustatory and kinaesthetic; which aligns with latest information collected from neurosciences where it is the recreation of the experiences.

[31] How we build memory is a fascinating story which involves an area of the brain

called hippocampus – I nicknamed it the "ear of the brain" for its shape and its role, as short-term memory will have to pass through it, before being stored as a long-term memory. One fascinating aspect of this is that the hippocampus is also our internal GPS, giving us the possibility to move through space and find the front from the back of a room. This may explain why memory seems to have a spatial location in our head, and the fact that all images we built have a spatial local. For a more in depth review of the various mechanisms of memories, you can start with the following post http://www.human-memory.net/processes_storage.html, we talked about types of memories, memory processes, short or long-term memory.

[32] This was the actual title of an article published in 1922, in the Journal of Philosophy – see below for the actual link to the page https://www.jstor.org/stable/2939648?seq=1#metadata_info_tab_contents

[33] From personal experience, story collected through a course in creative writing taken in Ireland, Dublin in 2004 (Dublin Writers Centre).

BIBLIOGRAPHY

Ashby, G. (2017). *The remarkable Learning Abilities of the Human Brain.* University of California Television, Series: "GRIT Talks" (uctv.tv).

Bach-y-Rita, P. *(1967). Sensory Plasticity.* Acta Neurologica Scandinavica.

Bateson, M. & Bateson, G. (2000). *Steps to an Ecology of Mind.* University of Chicago Press.

Borg, J. (2004). *Persuasion.* Harlow. Pearson Education Limited.

Bolstad, R. (2009). *Being At Cause In Your Life.* lifecoachpnlp.com/e01-being-at-cause.html

Burrows, C. (1996). *Automaticity of Social Behaviour: Direct Effects of Trait Construct and Stereotype Activation on Action.* www.yale.edu

Cameron-Bandler, L. & Lebeau, M. (1986). *The Emotional Hostage.* Real People Press.

Cuddy, A. (2012). *Your body language shapes who you are.* TED.com.

Deng, Y., Chang, L., Yang, M., Huo, M., Zhou, R. (2016). *Gender Differences in Emotional response: inconsistency between Experience and Expressivity.* PLoS ONE 11(6): e0158666.doi:10.1371/
journal.pone.015866 (plos.org).

Doidge, N. (2007). *The brain that changed itself.* Viking Press.

Dweck, C.S. (2006). *Mindset, the new psychology of success.* Random House.

Ekman, P. (2003). *Unmasking the Face: A Guide to Recognizing Emotions From Facial Expressions.* Malor Books

Ekman, P. (2014). *Darwin's claim of Universal in Facial Expressions Not Challenged.* Paul Ekman Group Ltd (paulekman.com/blog/darwins-claim-universals-facial-expression-challenged/).

Ekman, P. (2017). *The Atlas of Emotions.* Paul Ekman Group Ltd (atlasofemotions.org)

Feldman-Barrett, L. (2017). *You aren't at the mercy of your emotions – your brain creates them.* TED.com.

Goleman, D. (2004). *Destructive Emotions and how we can overcome them.* Bloomsbury Publishing Plc (Bloomsbury.com).

Hamilton, D. R. (2007). *Destiny vs. Free Will.* (Ed.) Hay House.

Hawkins, J. (2012). *How Brain science will change computing.* ted.com

Hodgkinson, G. P. & Healer, Mark P. (2011). *Psychological foundations of dynamic capabilities reflexion and reflection in strategic management.* Strategic Management Journal, 32, 1500–1516.

Hodgkinson, G. P., Langan-Fox, J., & Sadler-Smith, E. (2008). *Intuition: A fundamental bridging construct in the behavioural sciences.* British Journal of Psychology, 99, 1–27.

Hodgkinson, G. P, Sadler-Smith, E., Burke, L. A., Claxton, G. & Sparrow, P. R. (2009). *Intuition in Organizations: Implications for Strategic Management.* Long Range Planning, 42, 277–297.

(www.guyclaxton.com/documents/IntuitionwithEugenePaper09.pdf)

James, W. (1890). *The Principles of Psychology.* Henry Holt and Company (American Science Series – Advanced Course)

James, Drs T. & A. (2011). *NLP Practitioner and NLP Master Practitioner Course.* Tad James Co.

Jung, C. (1957, 2006). *The undiscovered self,* Signet Book.

Kahneman, D. (2013). *Thinking, Fast and Slow.* Farrar, Straus and Giroux.

Kahneman, D. (2010). *The riddle of experience vs memory.* TED.com.

Lakoff, G. & Johnson, M. (2003). *Metaphors you live by.* The University of Chicago Press Ltd.

Lawley, J. & Tompkins, P. (2000). *Metaphors in Mind: Transformation through Symbolic Modelling.* The Developing Company Press.

Maslow, A. H. (1943). *A theory of Human Motivation.* Archives Psychclassics.yorku.ca (Internet)

McCraty, R. (2015). *Science of the heart, Exploring the Role of the Heart in Human Performance.* HeartMath Institute (heartmath.com)

Oppezzo, M., Schwartz, D.L. (2014). *Give Your Ideas Some Legs: The Positive Effect of Walking on Creative Thinking,* Journal of Experimental Psychology: Learning, Memory, and Cognition, Vol. 40, No. 4, 1142-1152.

Peters, B.J., Overall, N.C., Jamieson, J.P. (2014). *Physiological and cognitive consequences of suppressing and expressing emotion in dyadic interactions.* Elsevier, International Journal of Psychophysiology 94 (available on psych.rochester.edu/research).

Ramachandran, V. (2009). *The neurons that shaped civilization.* TED.com.

Rees, J. & Sullivan, W. (2008). *Clean Language: Revealing Metaphors And Opening Minds.* Crown House Publishing Ltd.

Restak, R. (2004). *The New Brain: How the Modern Age is Rewiring Your Mind.* Rodale Books.

Salem, O. (2007). *The Heart, Mind and Spirit.* Royal College of Psychiatrists UK (rcpsych.ac.uk/).

Scott, J. (Various dates). *Collected Work.* CEOsage (scottjeffrey.com).

Shannon, C. (1948). *A mathematical theory of communication.* The Bell System Technical Journal (doi.org/10.1002/j.1538-7305.1948.tb01338.x).

The Human Memory. *Collected Work.* (human-memory.net).

Watt Smith, T. (2017). *The history of human emotions.* TED.com.

Wolpert, D. (2011). *The real reason for brains.* TED.com.

CONCLUSION

Here you are, swimming through the river, your first river ever.

Rough water or muddy water, whatever the situation, the swimming is not that different, rather always following the same principles,

> *going with the flow,*
>> *getting oxygen,*
>>> *admiring the landscape,*
>>>> *following the waves,*
>>>>> *at times in the waves,*
>>>>>> *at times surfing them.*

This is your first river ever.

> *And rivers pass through lakes, pass through mountains,*
>> *dives onto sea, dives onto oceans,*
>>> *travel the world, travel the universe,*

who knows

what hill will you be climbing next?

Printed in Great Britain
by Amazon